robate

| Lending Services | 552027 |
| 24hr Renewal Hotline | 552500 |

Please return/renew this item by the last date shown.
Thank you for using your library.

Wolverhampton Libraries

www.straightforwardco.co.uk

Straightforward Guides

© Straightforward Publishing 2019

British Cataloguing in Publication Data. A catalogue record is available for this book from the British library.

ISBN 978-1-84716-973-0

Printed by 4edge www.4edge.co.uk
Cover design by BW Studio Derby

Contents

Introduction

**

Introduction

This brief book, **updated to 2019**, outlines the important steps that needed to be taken when acting as an executor or administrator of an estate and also applying for probate and distributing the estate.

Death and dealing with death, particularly of a loved one or one who is very close, is an upsetting experience and needs to be dealt with sensitively. The last thing that most people want to deal with is the estate of the deceased person.

However, it is this aspect of death that causes the most problems in many cases. In a persons life there are many elements such as savings and investments, properties, pensions and other assets that accumulate. In many cases, when a person dies, no will has been left and it is down to friends and families to deal with these assets and to deal with the tax situation that may arise. Of course, life is easier if a will has been left spelling out who are the executors of the estate but even here the aftermath can be complicated.

This book will guide the reader through the five distinct stages: the meaning of probate; the will; actions pre-probate; applying for probate; distributing the estate. Although the stages are quite clear, quite often an individuals tax situation can be complicated. This aspect of probate is outlined in Chapter 4.

The book should prove useful to those who are in the process of dealing with the estate of a deceased person and hopefully make the whole situation clearer and less complicated.

In Scotland and Northern Ireland the procedures are slightly different to those in England and Wales, which this book mainly deals with. For more advice and guidance on probate and the law in Scotland you should go to:

www.scotcourts.gov.uk/taking-action/dealing-with-a-deceased's-estate-in-scotland

For Northern Ireland go to www.courtsni.gov.uk/en-GB/Services/Probate/Pages/ProbateInformation.aspx

**

Chapter 1

Probate Generally

What is probate?

When a person dies, it is necessary for someone to be appointed, with legal authority, to manage the deceased's financial affairs and wind up his/her estate. In law, the uncompleted financial matters of a deceased are known as 'the estate' and the person who is given the legal authority to wind up the estate is called the legal personal representative. After the application for probate, the document which proves the legal authority of the personal representative is called the grant of representation to an estate.

Where to get a grant of representation to an estate

Grants of representation to an estate are obtained from an office of the High Court known as the Probate Registry. The process of obtaining the grant is commonly known as 'probate'.

If someone leaves a will but dies without appointing an executor to carry out the terms of that will, or if the executors who are appointed by the will are unable or unwilling to carry out the duties of an executor, then the grant of representation obtained from the probate registry to prove that the will is a valid one and to authorize the person who obtains it to carry out its terms is called 'letters of administration with the will annexed'. If someone dies without making a will, that person dies intestate and the grant of representation obtained from the probate registry to authorize someone to wind up the estate is called 'letters of administration of the estate'. Those who obtain letters of administration are known as administrators of the estate. The main difference between the executor appointed under the will and the administrator of an estate are that an executors powers are given by the will and are more or less immediate whereas the administrators powers cannot be exercised until the Registry has appointed the administrator.

Essentially, probate and letters of administration can be seen as title documents to the assets of the deceased person's estate. However, there are a few assets where they are not required and can be dispensed with. These include what are known as nominated assets, jointly owned assets owned as joint tenants, estates of small value and estates which consist entirely of personal effects and/or personal currency. There may however still be a requirement to deal with HMRC in relation to inheritance tax. If in doubt contact the HMRC helpline 0300 123 1072 and outside UK 44+ 300 123 1072.

Property held jointly

Assets owned jointly are those that are not held in the sole name of the deceased. In English law, there are two ways of owning property jointly, either as joint tenants or tenants in common. In this sense, the word tenant doesn't mean tenant in the sense of landlord and tenant but is used universally in relationship to ownership of property.

If property is held as joint tenants the law clearly states that on the death of one of the owners, that person's share of the property does not become part of his estate (except for the purposes of Inheritance tax), it is inherited by the surviving joint owners, regardless of what is contained within the will. However, if property is held as tenants in common, the law states that on the death of one owner that persons share of the jointly owned property does become part of his or her estate.

The line between jointly owned property and property held as tenants in common is fine. However, there are a few obvious indicators. Usually, if bank or building society accounts are held jointly, along with stock and shares, they are considered joint tenancies. However, there has to be evidence of equal ownership of property. Any evidence to the contrary such as unequal payments, or sharing of rents, dividends etc, can mean tenancy in common.

Value of the estate-Estates valued under £15,000 gross

If the value of an estate before deducting the cost of the funeral and any debts left by the deceased is under £15,000, it is usually worth contacting organizations such as banks or building societies holding assets, to request that they make payment to the personal representative without going through the formalities of obtaining a grant of representation. They may or may not co-operate but it is worth contacting them. If the amounts involved are low then banks or building societies will co-operate on sight of a valid original will or if there is no will they will deal with the next of kin and a solicitor.

Obtaining a grant of representation and letters of administration

There are a number of main steps involved in obtaining probate or letters of administration with the will annexed or letters of administration and then administering the estate:

- Obtaining the information necessary to fill out the paperwork to obtain the grant of representation.
- preparing the documentation and then lodging the documentation to obtain an inheritance tax assessment and the issue of the grant of representation.
- Registering the grant in connection with the various assets and giving instructions as to how they are to be dealt with and collecting what is due to the estate.

Following the completion of the three main steps above there are a further three steps:

- Finalise the income and Capital gains tax positions
- Pay off the debts and discharge the liabilities of the estate.
- Distribute the remaining assets of the estate to the beneficiaries.

Dealing with the estate yourself or employing a solicitor

There are obvious advantages to using a solicitor. These are that solicitors are trained in law and can usually give sound guidance. They are usually necessary when it comes to complicated wills. They will take a lot of the work away from the executor which can be very helpful. They also have insurance to cover themselves against negligence. The obvious disadvantages can be the cost. Solicitors charge anything from between £150-250 per hour. In addition, a percentage charge can be made depending on the value of the estate. This is usually between 1-2% of the estate depending on value. If you intend to use a solicitor make sure you are fully acquainted with the costs before you instruct them to act.

Problems with personal representatives

In some cases, a will can specify an executor but that person is unwilling to act. Generally speaking, there is no legal obligation upon an executor or any other person entitled to apply for a grant of representation to apply for one. A person can give up their right to apply by signing a document to that effect, but this document is not binding until it is lodged with a probate registry.

When it has been lodged with a Registry he or she cannot then change their mind unless permitted by the court, which is rare. The only person who cannot refuse to take out a grant of representation is an executor of a will who has 'intermeddled' with an estate, which means someone who has already done something which shows an intention to act as executor or apply for a grant of probate.

Removing someone unsuitable to act

If a person who has already taken out a grant of representation to an estate behaves in a manner which is considered improper in relation to the estate or proves unsuitable in some other way, it is then usually possible to commence proceedings in a court to ask that he or she be removed from the position of personal representative and someone else replace him or her.

Stopping an application for a grant

If someone who is claiming an interest in an estate feels that an application has been made which should not be issued and he or she wants to make their views known to the registry, he or she can give notice to the registry that they wish to be heard before a grant is made. This notice, which is called a caveat, must be in writing and signed by the person issuing the notice.

This caveat will last for six months and while it is in force no grant of representation, other than one limited to the below can be made:

(overleaf)

- the administration of an estate until the conclusion of litigation currently taking place in the Chancery Division of the High Court in relation to the estate
- the preservation of an estate which will be endangered by delays in administering it.

****

Chapter 2

The Will

Who can wind up an estate?

To answer this question we need to go right back to the will, or the existence of a will or otherwise. Who will be entitled to wind up the estate depends on whether or not the deceased has left a valid will or codicil appointing an executor who is still living and prepared to act as an executor. A codicil is a document separate from the will but which is similarly signed and completed and annexed to the will and adds to or amends the will.

The existence of a will

There are several scenarios to consider here. If it is believed widely that the deceased person has made a will but the will cannot be found it may well have been lodged for safe keeping with the deceased's solicitor, bank or other person such as the accountant. If all enquiries draw a blank then enquiries can be made to the Record Keeper's Department at Principal Probate Registry, which is situated at 42-49 High Holborn, London WC1V 6NP Telephone (helpline) 0300 123 1072 (enquiries) 0207 421

8509-www.courttribunalfinder.service.gov.uk/court/london-probate-department. Wills can be deposited here for safe keeping. The Registry maintains an index of wills which is searched every time a grant of representation application is made. There are several websites in existence where it is possible to check the existence of a will, the main one being www.certainty.co.uk. (The National Will Register). If the will cannot be located it is sometimes possible to prove a will by a copy or by a reconstructed will if the original has been accidentally destroyed or lost. Obviously the evidence must be solid here in order to prove the authenticity of the will.

Is the will a valid document?

If a will is found then certain facts must be considered, such as whether the deceased person had the necessary legal capacity to make a will, whether the requisite formalities were complied with when the will was made, whether the will is valid or whether it has been revoked and to what property the will relates.

Capacity to make a will

For a will to be valid in this respect the person making the will (testator) must have the required degree of understanding to enter into the formation of a will. In other words, was that person of a sound mind? In England and Wales, The Mental Capacity Act 2005 contains a code of practice to help judges and others decide whether a person is of a sound mind. However, it is still the usual practice for the mental capacity to make a will to be decided by Common Law principles.

Under common law, to have testamentary capacity, in addition to being over the age of 18 (unless a seaman at sea or in the armed forces and on active military service), a testator must:

- be able to understand what making a will means
- be capable of having a rough idea of what he or she has to leave
- be aware of those who will benefit under the will
- understand, in broad terms the effect of the will without his or her decisions being affected by mental disorder.

A testator will be assumed to have testamentary capacity unless it is proved otherwise, and that the provisions of the will are not irrational to a degree that they don't make sense. As long as the person making the will was sane at the time of making it then the will should not be invalid if the testator becomes totally insane after making it.

The laws dealing with mental capacity are different in Scotland and Northern Ireland. In Scotland it is the Adults with Incapacity (Scotland) Act 2000 that is relevant and in Northern Ireland there is no equivalent.

The making of a valid will-Wills created outside England and Wales

If a will was made outside England and Wales then it will be valid under English law if it was made:

- in accordance with the laws of the country where it was made

- in accordance with the formalities required by the country where, at the time the will was made or at death, the Testator was domiciled or had his habitual residence or of which he was a national.

A will that was made on a ship or an aircraft is treated as validly completed if it was created in accordance with the law of the country with which the ship or aircraft has the closet connection, i.e. British Airways connected to Britain and so on.

Video Wills

Current legislation requires a Will to consist of "words in visible form" but a video recording may provide a suitable alternative. A video Will would be a unilateral declaration of the testator's wishes and, with video and audio to provide proof of identity, there would be no need for a signature. The video would also show capacity at the time of making the Will. Once more, storing the Will in a format that will not become inaccessible over time is a challenge that would need to be overcome. There is a further risk that the language used by the testator may not be sufficiently precise. A spoken Will would need to be well scripted in order to provide clear and complete instructions.

Wills which contain stipulations concerning property abroad

If the will deals with immoveable property such as a holiday home, it will be valid under English law if it complies with the formalities of the country in which it was made.

When drafting a will that deals with overseas property (any property) then it is necessary to consider the foreign law relating to property and the making of wills, even if the will was made in the United Kingdom. Some countries, such as France, are very different to the UK in their laws of inheritance. It will be necessary, if leaving property that is situated abroad to obtain advice from a lawyer who specializes in the law of that particular country.

Wills made by a member of the armed forces engaged in actual military service or a seaman at sea

There are very different laws relating to the above. If the will was made by a member of the armed forces engaged in actual military service or a seaman at sea then none of the usual formalities are required to be followed to make, or revoke, a will. These wills can be made irrespective of age, do not have to be in writing, can be made orally provided that the intention is that the conversation shall have testamentary effect. If the will is written, it does not have to be witnessed, and the will is not revoked by lapse of time or a return to civilian life (or in the case of a seaman, to land).

Wills made in England and Wales

If a will made in England or Wales (other than servicemen as discussed above) is to be seen as a valid will, then certain formalities have to be complied with:

- The will must be in writing. Any form of writing is valid, but it must be in writing. (but see previous paragraph about video wills)

- The will must have been signed and witnessed. To date, electronic signatures are not accepted. The person signing the will can be someone at the testator's request.

- The will must be witnessed by two or more people who are present at the same time. The witnesses must be of age and mentally capable of witnessing a will. Each witness must have signed the will and either signed or acknowledged his signature in the testators presence.

- It must be apparent that the testator intended to give effect to the will by signing it. In practice the signatures of all concerned will be entered at the end of the will.

The revoking of wills

Those engaged in actual military service and seamen at sea can revoke a will at any age, orally and without formalities. Also, If a person marries or remarries or goes through a civil partnership ceremony after the date of making a will, the will is revoked, unless the will is made with that particular marriage or civil partnership in mind and was intended to remain in force after the event. Any appointment of property made by will in the exercise of a power of appointment that the testator has will not be revoked if he subsequently enters into a civil partnership (unless the property would form part of his estate if he had not made the appointment).

Revocation by destruction with intention to revoke

A will is revoked if it was destroyed by a testator or by another person at his request and in his presence. In either case, the testator must have intended that the will should be revoked.

However, central to this is the fact that for the whole will to be revoked then this should be apparent and obvious. If the will was only partially destroyed or obliterated for example by tearing a piece out, then this will not revoke the whole will.

The creation of a new will, or revocation by codicil

A new will, or a codicil which contains a clause which states that any previous will is revoked will be effective. If there is a later will containing no revocation clause but which contains provisions inconsistent with a previous will, the provisions of the earlier will which are inconsistent with the new provisions are considered to be revoked. However, all other provisions of the earlier will are effective.

Alterations and obliterations to a will

Alterations, obliterations or insertions in a will or codicil are of no effect if not signed and witnessed in the same way as the whole will.

The effect of divorce or annulment of marriage or dissolution of a civil partnership on a will

Dissolution of any of the above does not invalidate a will, but a decree absolute (not a decree nisi) makes any provisions in a will appointing a spouse or a civil partner as a trustee or executor, or conferring powers of appointment on the spouse or civil partner, invalid. The effect is as if the former spouse or civil partner had died on the day that the decree became absolute. In the same way, a decree absolute makes any bequest in the will to the spouse or civil partner take effect as if the former spouse or civil partner had died on the same day the decree becomes absolute, leaving bequests in the remainder of the will valid.

Usually the bequest will become part of the residue of the estate and be inherited by the residuary beneficiaries, but if the bequest is of the entire estate or of a share of the residue of the estate, it will be treated as not having been disposed of by the will and will be inherited on death according to the laws of intestacy.

Valid wills appointing an under-age executor

If the deceased person has left a valid will or codicil that is relevant to property in England or Wales, the people with the first right to deal with or administer the estate are the executors appointed by the will or codicil. However, if the person appointed is under the age of 18, he or she cannot act although the High Court can appoint the parents or a guardian or other person to act until he or she becomes of age.

Executors who do not wish to act or who wish to delay acting

Even though a person has been named in a will as an executor he or she is not obliged to do so and can sign a form of renunciation giving up the right to the executorship providing that this is done before any rights of executor are exercised. If one appointed executor renounces the right then the other appointed executor can proceed to obtain a grant of probate solely.

An executor who renounces executorship should pass all forms signed to the co-executor(s) or if no other executor is prepared to prove the will then to the person entitled to letters of administration of the estate with the will annexed. An executor who wishes to renounce his right to probate but who cannot find his co-executor or the next person in line to prove the will or entitled to letters of administration of the estate can discharge himself and obtain a receipt by lodging the appropriate documentation such as the form of renunciation at any district probate registry.

If a person wishes to delay his power to act, for whatever reason, allowing the other executors to go ahead, he can reserve the power to prove the will till a later date. This again is done by lodging the appropriate documentation at the probate registry.

If no suitable executor is appointed

If an executor is considered to be unsuitable to act, a court can be requested to remove that person from office and appoint someone else in place. In exercising discretion to appoint or remove personal representatives the court will attach importance to the wishes of the beneficiaries.

If all the executors are unable or unwilling to act, or if the will or codicil has not given anyone the position of executor, or if a court removes the only remaining executor, member of the below groups of people are entitled to apply for a grant of letters of administration with the will annexed:

1. Those entitled (on trust for any other person) to that part of the estate which remains after taking out any specific gifts or legacies made by the will (residue of the estate).
2. Those entitled to the residue of the estate.
3. If the residue is not fully disposed of then those entitled to the part left.
4. The personal representatives of the above (3).
5. Any legatee or creditor of the deceased.
6. The personal representatives of the above (5).

Only when there is no member of a group who is willing to take out a grant is a member of the next group considered.

If there is no valid will

In many cases, unfortunately, there is no valid will and complications arise. If there is no valid will, the following are entitled to wind up the estate:

- Husband or wife or registered civil partner.
- Sons or daughters or their descendants.
- Parents.
- Brothers or sisters of the whole blood, or their descendants.
- Brothers or sisters of the half blood, or their descendants.
- Grandparents.
- Uncles and aunts of the whole blood or descendants.
- Uncles or aunts of the half blood or their descendants.
- The Crown.
- Creditors of the deceased.

Only blood or adoptive relationships count, not step relations.

The number of personal representatives

Not more than four people can obtain grant of representation from a probate registry to act at the same time, even if a will is complex and appoints separate executors for different parts of the estate, such as literary executors, general executors etc.In the case of letters of administration, the grant is usually given to the first of those equally entitled to apply, but if there is a dispute between them as to whom the grant should be given, the registry will favour those it considers are the most likely the estate the most effectively (to the best advantage of the beneficiaries and the creditors).

Calls to rewrite Victorian laws on will making

The Law Commission announced, on July 13th 2017, the launching of a consultation paper looking at the whole process of making a will, including allowing for them to be written electronically and by people as young as 16. They announced that the current legislation is out of step with the modern world and puts people off making a will.

An estimated 40 per cent of people die without making a will, which means that there is no guarantee that their estates are distributed as they wish. People are also ignorant of the law. The Commission also notes the significant variation in the age at which people can make a will in different jurisdictions. In Scotland for example, a person over the age of 12 can make a valid will. For more information on this go to: https://www.lawgazette.co.uk/law/law-commission-proposes-wide-reaching-wills-overhaul.

Chapter 3

Initial Steps after Death-The Role and Responsibilities of Executors Pre-Probate

___

The formalities

Relatives or friends of the deceased will take on the task of dealing with the necessary formalities after death. In the first instance, notwithstanding where the person dies, a doctor must provide relatives with a certificate stating the cause of death. This certificate is then lodged at the Registry of Births Deaths and Marriages within five days of the issue. The registrar will need to know full details of the death and will also ask for any other certificates such as marriage and birth. The person who registers the death is known as the 'informant'.

If the doctor states that the cause of death is uncertain, then the arrangements are rather more complex. The death will first be reported to the coroner, who usually orders a post-mortem. If it shows that the cause of death was natural, the coroner then authorises the burial or cremation. In these cases, you will be issued with a death certificate by the Registrar and a second certificate permitting the undertaker to arrange burial or cremation.

Except in rare cases, for example violent death when the coroner orders an inquest to be held, it will now be time to organise the funeral. It will be necessary at this point to check the will or if there is no will, to find out about the arrangements for administering the estate.

If the death occurred when the deceased was abroad and it was registered with the British Consulate copies of the death certificate can be obtained from the consulate, or the Overseas Registration Section, General Register Office, Smedleys Hydro, Trafalgar Road, Birkdale, Southport PR8 2HH. 0300 123 1837.

Funeral arrangements

Search for any document which may indicate the wishes of the deceased in relation to their funeral. Muslims and Orthodox Jews are usually buried and Hindus are cremated. Sikhs request cremation and that their ashes are scattered in a river or the sea. Non-Orthodox Jews sometimes request cremation and some Christians prefer burial and others cremation. If a 'Green' funeral is required the natural death centre can supply further information. In practice, the family usually arranges the funeral. They can be contacted at naturaldeath.org.uk 01962 712 690.

If there is a will in existence, it may well contain details concerning the desired funeral arrangements of the deceased. If there are no clear instructions the executors of the will usually make appropriate arrangements. The executor will become legally liable to pay costs of the funeral.

Where the deceased dies intestate, the 'administrators' of the estate will instruct the undertaker and assume responsibility for payments. In some cases, it may be clear that the deceased does not have enough assets to cover the funeral. If this is the case then investigations need to take place, including the possibility of a one-off funeral grant to cover costs. Once financial details have been settled it is advisable to put a notice in the deaths column of one or more papers to bring the funeral to the attention of relatives.

The responsibilities of executors

Executors and administrators of estates have very important responsibilities. In the first instance they are responsible for ensuring that the assets of the estate are paid to the correct beneficiaries of the will and also for ensuring that all debts are paid before distribution.

If this aspect of administration is mismanaged then the executor or administrator will be held, or could be held, liable for any debts. In order to ensure that they are protected then executors or administrators should advertise in the London Gazette – which is a newspaper for formal notices of any kind, and also a local paper together with requests that creditors should submit their claims by a date which must be at least two months after the advertisement. Private individuals will usually have to produce a copy of probate before their advertisement is accepted for publication.

See sample letters to the London Gazette and local newspapers in Appendix one.

The executor's initial steps

If you are the executor of a valid will (or if you are the administrator if there is no will) you can now begin the task of administering the estate.

It will be essential to ensure that the basic elements are dealt with such as informing utilities, arranging for termination of certain insurance policies and discharge of liabilities of others such as life insurance. Arrangements will need to be made for any pets and post redirected. Valuables that can be stolen should be removed from the building for safekeeping. All licences, such as television licences, car tax and any other necessary licences should be returned and refunds obtained. Arrangements should be made with the post office to redirect mail. Anyone else with a connection to the deceased who may be receiving a benefit, or, for example, may be renting a property from the deceased, has to be notified. If there are tenants then all future rents should be paid to the executor or proposed administrator of the estate. These are the basic essential lifestyle elements before you make an application for probate.

The value of the estate

Before you can apply for probate of the will, you have to find out the extent and value of the assets and liabilities of the estate. You will need to have access to all records of assets, such as insurance policies and bank accounts. The ease with which you can establish a total value will depend on how organised the deceased was. If the deceased was a taxpayer it is advisable to approach the local tax office for a copy of his or her last tax return, sending a copy of the will to prove your status as an executor.

Once you have collated all proof of assets including property you will need to arrive at a total value. The following will provide a pointer for establishing value:

Bank accounts

Interest-bearing accounts and joint bank accounts

When you have found out details of these accounts you should ask for details of balance and accrued interest at the time of death. This is needed for the tax return you will have to complete on behalf of the deceased's estate.

These types of accounts can be problematic. If the joint holders are husband and wife, the account will pass automatically to the survivor. In other cases you will need to establish the intentions of the joint owners or the contribution of each to the joint account. This is because the amount contributed by the deceased forms part of the estate for tax purposes (except where a written agreement confirms that the money in the account passes automatically to the survivor). In the case of business partnership accounts, you need a set of final trading accounts to the date of death and should contact the surviving partner.

See example letters to banks and building society in appendix one.

National Savings

These may take the form of National Savings Certificates, National Savings Investment Accounts or Premium Bonds. A claim form for repayment should be obtained, usually from the post office and sent to the appropriate department for National Savings together with a copy of the probate when you have it.

Building societies

You would approach a building society in the same way as a bank, asking for a balance and interest to date. You should also ask for a claim form for payment.

Life insurance

You should write to insurance companies stating the date of death and the policy number and enclose a copy of the death certificate. Once probate has been obtained submit your claim form for monies owed. In many cases, policies are held on trust and will not form part of an estate. Insurance companies will, on production of the death certificate, make payment direct to the beneficiaries.

Stock and shares

You should make arrangements to forward a list of stocks and shares held by the deceased to a bank or stockbroker. In the case of ISA's you should send them to the plan manger and ask for a valuation. Ask for transfer forms for all shareholdings. You may decide to value the stocks and shares yourself. If this is the case, you will need a copy of the official Stock Exchange Daily Official List for the day on which the deceased died. The valuation figure is calculated by adding 25% of the difference between the selling and buying prices. If the death took place at the weekend you can choose either the Monday or Friday Valuation. However, if the executors sell any shares at a loss within 12 months, the selling price in all cases can be taken as the value at the date of death.

If you cannot locate all of the share certificates, you may be able to find dividend counterfoils or tax vouchers among the papers of the deceased which will enable you to check the number of shares held in the company. If you cannot find share certificates, write to the Registrar of the company. Name of Registrars are given in the Register of Registrars held in the local library. The same approach can be made if the deceased holds unit trusts. In the case of private companies where no value of shares is published, you may sometimes be able to obtain a valuation from the secretary of the company. In the case of a family company it will usually be necessary to have the value determined by a private accountant.See sample letter in Appendix one.

The employer

If the deceased was employed, then it will be necessary to send a letter to the employer informing them of the death and also requesting details of any salaries owed, pension companies etc. See sample letter in Appendix one.

Pensions

If the deceased was already receiving a pension, you should write to the company operating the scheme in order to find out further details, i.e. is the pension paid up until the time of death, are there any other beneficiaries after death and so on. Pensions vary significantly and it is very important that accurate information is obtained.

See sample letter in Appendix one.

State benefits

If the deceased was in receipt of an old age pension, notice of the death should be given to the Department of Work and Pensions, so that any adjustments can be made. In the case of married men, the agency will make arrangements to begin to pay widows pension.

Businesses

The valuation of a business on the death of one of the partners is complicated and depends upon the nature of the business, the way in which the accounts are prepared and the extent of the assets held by the business. The surviving partner/s should make available a set of partnership accounts to the date of death and help you to determine the correct valuation for the deceased share.

Farms

If the deceased had an interest in a farm, any type of farm you should seek advice of a more specialist agricultural valuer.

Residential property

If the estate is below the inheritance tax threshold (£325,000 2019/2020), you may be able to estimate the value of the property by looking at similar properties in estate agents windows. You may also wish to obtain a professional valuation. If the estate reaches the inheritance tax threshold or is close to it, the figure is checked by the District Valuer. If the property is sold within four years of death for less than the probate valuation, and providing the sellers are executors and not beneficiaries, the sale price may be substituted for the original valuation.

In the case of joint properties, the value of the person who has died forms part of the estate for tax purposes. However, if the share passes to the spouse, the 'surviving spouse exemption' applies. This means that there is no inheritance tax to pay, even if the estate exceeds the inheritance tax threshold. If there is a mortgage on the property at the date of death, the amount of the debt must be found by writing to the bank or building society. The value of the house is reduced by this amount. Where the deceased has left residential property as a specific item, the will may either say that the property is to be transferred to the beneficiary free from any mortgage or that it is subject to a mortgage, The Administration of Estates Act 1925 provides that a person who is bequeathed a mortgaged property is responsible repaying the mortgage unless the will sets out a contrary intention.

Other property and buildings

If the deceased owned commercial property, the executor has to determine whether this was a business asset or whether it is an investment property unconnected with any business. If this is the case a separate valuation will be needed.

Personal possessions

Although it is not always necessary to obtain professional valuations for household goods, estimated values are examined very carefully by the District Valuer if the estate is large enough to attract inheritance tax. The way household goods are dealt with will depend entirely on their value. In certain cases, with items such as painting and jewellery then an auction may be appropriate.

Income tax

It is very unlikely that, before you make your application for probate, you will be in a position to calculate the income tax owed on an estate. As the administration of the estate gathers momentum then you will amass enough information to start forming a picture of the value and thus the tax liabilities.

See sample letter in Appendix one.

Chapter 4

Making the Application for Probate

___

Applying for Probate

Probate represents the official proof the validity of a will and is granted by the court on production by the executors of the estate of the necessary documents. Only when probate is obtained are executors free to administer and distribute the estate. If the value of the estate is under £5000 in total, it may be possible to administer the estate without obtaining probate. Generally, if the estate is worth more than £5000, you will have to apply for probate of the will or letters of administration. There are a number of reasons for this:

- Banks, building societies and National Savings are governed by the Administration of Estates (Small payments) Act 1965. This only allows them to refund individual accounts up to £5000 without production of probate.

- You cannot sell stocks, shares or land from an estate without probate, except in the case of land held in names of joint tenants where this passes on after death If the administration is disputed or if a person intends to make a claim as a dependant or member of the family, his or her claim is 'statute barred' six months after the grant of probate. The right to take action remains open if the estate is administered without probate

- A lay executor who managed to call in the assets of an estate without probate might miss the obligation to report matters to HMRC for inheritance tax purposes, especially where a substantial gift had been made in the seven years prior to the death.

Letters of administration

If someone dies intestate (without making a will) the rules of intestacy laid down by Act of Parliament will apply. An administrator must apply for letters of administration for exactly the same reasons as the executor applies for probate. The grant of letters of administration will be made to the first applicant. If a will deals with part only but not all of the administration (for example where the will defines who receives what but does not name an executor) the person entitled to apply for letters of administration makes the application to the Registrar attaching the will at the same time. The applicant is granted 'Letters of administration with will attached'.

Applying for letters of administration

The following demonstrates the order of those entitled to apply:

- The surviving spouse/civil partner (not unmarried partner)
- The children or their descendants (once over 18)
- If there are no children or descendants of those children who are able to apply, the parents of the deceased can apply
- Brothers and sisters 'of the half blood'
- Grandparents
- Aunts and uncles of the whole blood
- Aunts and uncles of the half blood
- The Crown (or Duchy of Lancaster or Duchy of Cornwall) if there are no blood relations.

Where the estate is insolvent other creditors have the right to apply.

The Probate Registry – applying for probate

The first step is to obtain the necessary forms from the personal application department of the Principal Probate Registry in

London or the local district probate registry. The more straightforward cases can usually be handled by post or by one visit to the probate registry. There is also the facility to carry out the probate function online. The executor will complete and send in the forms, they are checked and the amount of probate fees and inheritance tax assessed. The registry officials prepare the official document which the executor then swears, attending personally to do so. The process from submission to swearing usually takes three to four weeks.

Filling in the forms

The necessary forms for applying for probate can be obtained from the probate registry. These are:

- Form PA1P – the probate application form if person left a will
- Form PA1A if person did not leave a will
- Form 1HT 205 – the return of assets and debts

Examples of these forms are shown in Appendix three.

However, see below for more complicated estate returns.

With the forms you will receive other items which serve as guidance to the forms and process:

- 1HT 206 – notes to help you with 1HT 205
- Form PA3 – a list of probate fees
- Form PA4 – Directory of Probate Registries

Form PA1P is fairly uncomplicated. The form is split into white and blue sections with the applicant filling in the white sections. The form will ask which office the applicant wants to attend, details of the deceased, the will and something about you. In cases where more than one executor is involved, the registrar will usually correspond with one executor only. The form also has a space for naming any executors who cannot apply for probate, e.g. because they do not want to or have died since the will was written. If they may apply at a later date, the probate office will send an official 'power reserved letter' which the non-acting executor signs. This is a useful safeguard in case the first executor dies or becomes incapacitated before grant of probate is obtained.

You do not have to sign form PA1P. At the end of the process, the probate registry will couch the information you supply in legal jargon for the document you are required to sign.

Form PA1P contains a reminder that you have to attach the death certificate, the will and the completed IHT form. If this form demonstrates that the estate exceeds the 'excepted estate' threshold (for inheritance tax purposes) form 1HT 200 will have to be completed.

Procedure for obtaining probate where the tax situation is more complicated

Although the procedure for obtaining a grant of probate, a grant of letters of administration or a grant of letters of administration with will annexed are similar, the procedure concerning inheritance tax accounts is rather more complicated.

There are three types of inheritance tax account, with different forms in each case. They are as follows:

1. If the deceased lived abroad and he or she has few assets in the UK, then form IHT207 will usually be the one to use. In some cases form IHT 400 must be used but form IHT 207 will make this clear.
2. If the deceased was domiciled in the United Kingdom then form IHT 205 is the usual form to use where:

the gross value of the estate does not exceed the excepted estate limit, which is the inheritance tax threshold (currently £325,000) unless a grant of probate is applied for before 6th of August in the tax year in which the death took place, in which case the excepted estate limit is the inheritance tax limit set for the previous tax year

1) the Chancellor announced, in the July 2015 budget, that he was increasing the IHT allowance to £1m (for a couple) for the family home. People will not have to pay IHT on properties worth less than £1million. This was phased in from April 2017. However, there are a few things to note. The 'Family Homes Allowance' applies only to property left to direct descendants, children, grandchildren, great grandchildren and so on. Stepchildren will also count. The allowance will not apply to indirect descendants such as nieces and nephews. It is also suggested that advice should be sought when thinking of downsizing as the new IHT rules may affect your tax liabilities.

- the gross value is not more than £100,000 and there is no tax to pay after taking into account the value of the assets inherited by exempt bodies, such as charities or the deceased's spouse or civil partner, if the deceased and the spouse or civil partner were both born in the United Kingdom and were domiciled here throughout their lives

Recent developments

Since April 2018, anyone leaving a home, or a share of a home, to direct descendants (children, grandchildren etc) is entitled to an additional Inheritance Tax exemption of up to £150,000. This increases to £175,000 in April 2020.

The gross value of a person's estate is the total value of his assets together with the value of any gifts made by him (a) in the seven years before his death or (b) from which he continued to benefit and upon which he had elected not to pay the pre-owned assets income tax charge or (c) from which he had reserved a benefit.

Form IHT 400 should be used if:

- the deceased was domiciled in the United Kingdom but his estate does not fall within the above classes
- the estate includes an alternatively secured
- pension, that is, a pension benefit in a pension scheme registered under section 153 of the

Finance Act 2004 which has been earmarked to provide benefits for a person over the age of 75 but not used to provide pension benefits or an annuity for him

- the deceased had an unsecured benefit from a pension scheme registered under section 153 of the Finance Act 2004 and he acquired the benefit as a dependent of a person who died aged 75 or over

- the deceased had not taken his full retirement benefits before he died from a personal pension policy or a pension scheme of which he was a member and when he was in poor health, he changed the policy or scheme so as to make a change in or to dispose of the benefits to which he was entitled

- the deceased ever bought an annuity and within seven years of his death paid premiums for a life assurance policy of which the policy monies were not payable to his estate, his spouse or civil partner

- the deceased had a right to benefit from assets held in a trust (other than assets held in a single trust which do not exceed £150,000)

- within seven years of his death the deceased gave up a right to benefit from assets valued at more than £150,000 held in trust

- within seven years of his death the deceased made gifts (other than normal birthday, festive, marriage or civil partnership gifts not exceeding £3000 per year) totaling over £150,000

- the deceased made a gift after 18th March 1986 from which he continued to benefit or in respect of which the person who received the gift did not take full possession of it

- the deceased had made an election that the pre-owned assets income charge should not apply to assets he had previously owned or to the cost of which he had contributed and in either case from which he had continued to benefit

- the deceased lived abroad and form IHT 207 is not appropriate

- the deceased owned or benefited from assets outside the United Kingdom worth more than £100,000

- the estate intends to claim and benefit from any unused nil-rate inheritance tax band of a spouse or civil partner who has died before the deceased (this is done by completing form IHT 402 and returning it with the completed form IHT 400.

For more details about IHT 400 go to:

www.gov.uk/government/publications/inheritance-tax-inheritance-tax-account-iht400

Distributing an estate in accordance with the law of intestacy
If someone dies without making a will he is said to die intestate and his estate is inherited according to the law of intestacy. Intestacy law divides relatives into groups or classes according to their blood relationships to the deceased. All members of a given class inherit in equal shares. There is a specific order in which the various classes inherit and if all members of a given class have died before the deceased without leaving issue who survived the deceased, the next class inherits. The words 'child' and 'children' are used to mean a persons immediate dependents (as opposed to grandchildren) and do not include a stepchild or stepchildren, but no distinction is made before legitimate and illegitimate children. Adopted children inherit from their adoptive parents and not from their birth parents.

If those entitled to inherit are under 18, then the inheritance is held in trust for them, until they either reach the age of 18, marry or enter into a registered civil partnership.

To decide who is entitled to inherit, look for the first class and if there is no member of the class who survived the deceased or predeceased him look for those in the next class.

The law of intestacy (See appendix 1 for intestacy flowchart)

If a person dies without leaving a will or without leaving a valid will, the laws of intestacy apply. It is important to note that the Inheritance and Trustees Power Act 2014 has introduced changes regarding who will inherit under and intestate estate and also how much they inherit. The changes will have no effect on people who die with assets worth less than £250,000.

The law of intestacy rests on the question of: who survived the deceased? If there is a lawful spouse or civil partner and the deceased died leaving children then the spouse receives the first £250,000 in respect of assets solely in the deceased's name plus half of the remaining capital. Children receive half remaining capital, then on the death of the spouse/civil partner the children receive the remaining capital.

If there is a lawful spouse/civil partner and the deceased died leaving no children, the spouse receives the entire estate. This is a new provision introduced following the introduction of the above mentioned Inheritance and Trustees Powers Act 2014, which came into force in October 2014. The changes apply in England and Wales.

If there are children, but no spouse or civil partner, everything goes to the children in equal shares.

If there are parent(s) but no spouse or civil partner or children then everything goes to parents in equal shares.

If there are brothers or sisters, but no spouse or civil partner, or children or parents everything goes to brothers and sisters of the whole blood equally.

If there are no brothers or sisters of the whole blood, then all goes to brothers and sisters of the half blood equally.

If there are grandparents, but no spouse or civil partner, or children or parents, or brothers and sisters everything goes to the grandparents equally.

If there are uncles and aunts, but no spouse or civil partner, or children or parents, or brothers or sisters or grandparents, then everything goes to uncles and aunts of the whole blood equally.

If there are no uncles and aunts of the whole blood, then all goes to uncles and aunts of the half blood equally.

If there is no spouse or civil partner and no relatives in any of the categories shown above then everything goes to the Crown. A spouse is a person who was legally married to the deceased when he or she died.

A civil partner is someone who was in a registered civil partnership with the deceased when he or she died. It doesn't include people simply living together as unmarried partners or as common law husband and wife.

The term children includes children born in or out of wedlock and legally adopted children; it also includes adult sons and daughters. It does not, however, include stepchildren.

Brothers and sisters of the whole blood have the same mother and father. Brothers and sisters of the half blood (more

58

commonly referred to as half brothers and sisters) have just one parent in common.

Uncles and aunts of the whole blood are brothers and sisters of the whole blood of the deceased's father or mother.

Uncles and aunts of the half blood are brothers and sisters of the half blood of the deceased's father or mother.

It is important to note that if any of the deceased children die before him, and leave children of their own (that is grandchildren of the deceased) then those grandchildren between them take the share that their mother or father would have taken if he or she had been alive. This also applies to brothers and sisters and uncles and aunts of the deceased who have children – if any of them dies before the deceased, the share that he or she would have had if he or she were still alive, goes to his or her children between them.

The principle applies through successive generations – for example a great grandchild will take a share of the estate if his father and his grandfather (who were respectively the grandson and son of the deceased) both died before the deceased.

It is important to note that if any of the following situations apply to you, or if you are in any doubt whatsoever, you should seek legal advice before distributing the estate of a person who has died without leaving a will:

- The deceased died before 4th of April 1988
- Anyone entitled to a share of the estate is under 18
- Someone died before the deceased and the share he or she would have had goes to his or her children instead
- The spouse/civil partner dies within 28 days of the deceased.

A spouse or civil partner must outlive the deceased by 28 days before they become entitled to any share of the estate. An ex-wife or civil partner (who was legally divorced from the deceased or whose civil partnership with the deceased was dissolved before the date of death) gets nothing from the estate under the rules of intestacy, but he/she may be able to make a claim under the inheritance (Provision for Family and Dependants) Act 1975, through the courts. Legal advice should be sought if making such a claim. Anyone who is under 18 (except a spouse or civil partner of the deceased) does not get his or her share of the estate until he or she becomes 18, or marries under that age. It must be held on trust for him or her until he or she becomes 18 or gets married. Apart from the spouse or civil partner of the deceased, only blood relatives, and those related by legal adoption, are entitled to share in the estate. Anyone else who is related through marriage and not by blood is not entitled to a share in the estate.

If anyone who is entitled to a share of the estate dies after the deceased but before the estate is distributed, his or her share forms part of his or her own estate and is distributed under the terms of his or her will or intestacy. Great uncles and great aunts of the deceased (that is brothers and sisters of his or her grandparents) and their children are not entitled to a share in the estate.

Further changes under the Inheritance and Trustees Powers Act 2014

The definition of personal property/chattels has also changed. Under old rules, the term "chattels" was outdated and included old-fashioned terms such as "carriages", "linen" and "scientific instruments". Under new rules "personal chattels" includes all tangible moveable property, apart from property which consists of money or security for money, or property that was used solely or mainly for business purposes or was held solely as an investment. The old definition of chattels will still apply where a Will was executed before 1 October 2014 and makes reference to s55 (1) (x) (Administration of Estates Act 1925). Under old rules, if an individual died leaving a child under the age of 18, who was subsequently adopted by someone else, there was a risk that the child may lose their inheritance from their natural parent. The new rules ensure that children will not lose any claim to inheritance if they were adopted after the death of a natural parent.

Various points concerning distributions of the estate

Children conceived by artificial insemination or in vitro fertilisation

When distributing to those known to have been conceived by artificial insemination or by in vitro fertilisation the following should be borne in mind: Except for inheritance of titles and land which devolves with titles, if a child is artificially conceived as above:

- In the case of a couple who are married and not judicially separated, the husband is considered to be the father unless it can be proved that he did not consent to the conception

- In the case of treatment provided for a man and woman together, the man is considered to be the father irrespective of whether or not his sperm was used

- The mother is the woman who has carried the child as the result of the placing in her of an embryo or of an egg or sperm.

Although the Human Fertilisation and Embryology (Deceased Fathers) Act 2003 permits a deceased husband or partner to be registered as the father of a child conceived after his death by the use of his sperm, the registration does not give the child any rights of inheritance.

Underage beneficiaries

Unless permitted to do so by the will, neither a person under the age of 18 nor that persons parent or guardian can give a valid receipt for the capital of the bequest (as opposed to the income that it produces) and cannot give a valid discharge for any capital payment made to him. A valid receipt for income produced by a bequest to a person who is under the age of 18 can only be given by the person, or his parent or guardian, if the beneficiary is married or in a registered civil partnership. Accordingly, a personal representative should not make any capital payment to a minor, or an income payment to an unmarried minor who is not in a registered civil partnership unless authorised by the will. The money should be either held on trust until of age or paid into court.

Bankrupts and those of unsound mind

Payments should not be made to a beneficiary who is bankrupt. Similarly, if a bequest has been made to a person who is not believed to be of sound mind, the bequest should not be made to that person personally but to his deputy appointed by the court of protection or to his attorney appointed by an enduring power of attorney made by him before 1st October 2007 or a lasting power of attorney. In the case of both types of power of attorney the powers must have been registered with the Public Guardian and made before the beneficiary lost his sanity.

Beneficiaries who cannot be found

There may be cases where it is difficult to trace a beneficiary, even though every effort may have been made, such as advertising in the local paper or even national papers. If executors do not personally know a beneficiaries address or whereabouts then other exhaustive searches will have to be made, such as the local telephone directory where the beneficiary lives There are other avenues which can be explored.

One is that of Traceinline on 02392 988 966 www.traceinline.co.uk. They can trace beneficiaries if the executor can supply the person's name and date of birth. A fee is payable. Traceline will also inform the executor if the beneficiary has died. There is a fee to be paid so it is only worth it if there is significant money and assets at stake.

Probate Fees

The fee for initial probate is £215, although there is no fee if the estate is valued at less than £5,000. You must enclose a cheque for the application fee if applying by post. You can pay for extra official copies of the grant of representation, which may be used to send to institutions in place of the original grant (an ordinary copy is not acceptable for this purpose).

The fee for each official copy is 50p a copy if you request it with the application.

*

Probate online

The Probate Service is now accepting online applications from personal applicants and a small number of pre-selected solicitors based on the criteria below:

- applications where up to 4 executors are applying
- there is an original will available even if the person who died made changes to that will (these changes are known as codicils)
- the person who has died classed England and Wales as their permanent home or intended to return to England and Wales to live permanently.
- The online application form will continue to be developed to cover a broader range of probate applications in the future.

What the new online application provides

The new online application form includes:

- a new statement of truth for you to declare that the information provided is correct, which removes the need for you to swear an oath in person
- the function to pay the fee online removing the need to post a cheque to the Probate Service

- a 'save and return' function allows you to save and revisit an application if you need to find further information. This allows a part finished application to be saved and completed later.

What is required in order to submit an online application?

The online application form is easier to understand but you will still be required to provide supporting documents as per the current process. These are:

- the original will and two photocopies
- an official copy of the death certificate
- the associated inheritance tax forms and figures
- any other supporting documents relevant to the case (e.g. a renunciation form)

The government is are looking to enhance this in the future, potentially through links with other departments to gather this information automatically as part of the process. If you meet the criteria, you can apply online.

Alternatively - Sending the forms

If the estate you are administering can be contained on form 1HT 205, you are ready to send in your application. Make sure that you take photocopies of all material. You should send the following:

- The will
- The death certificate
- Probate application form PA1P or PA1A
- Short form 1HT 205
- A cheque for the fee

Attach any explanatory letter as necessary. You should then send the package by registered post. A few weeks later, you will be invited to review the documents, pay the probate fee and swear the prescribed oath. Remember to take your file of background papers.

Probate fees are calculated on the amount of the net estate, as declared for the purpose of inheritance tax. Fees are payable when you attend the interview at the registry – see form PA3 for guidance.

Attendance at the probate registry

When you arrive at the probate registry you will need to examine the forms that have been prepared for you. You need to satisfy yourself that all the details are correct. When you have checked all the details, the commissioner will ask you to sign the original will and swear the oath, identifying the will as that of the deceased. The actual process entails you standing up, holding a copy of the New Testament and repeating the words spoken by the commissioner. The words take the form of 'I swear by Almighty God that this is my name and handwriting and that the contents of this my oath are true and that this is the will referred to'. The form of oath is varied depending on religious belief or otherwise.

The commissioner will then sign beneath your signature on the official form and will. The fees are paid and any sealed copies as ordered will be supplied.

Letters of administration

If the deceased has left no will, then the next of kin will apply for a grant of letters of administration instead of probate. The same is the case if a will was left but no executors appointed. In these cases, the grant is called 'letters of administration with will annexed'

When letters of administration are sought, the administrators may in some cases have to provide a guarantee – for example where the beneficiaries are under age or mentally disabled or when the administrator is out of the country. The guarantee is provided by an insurance company at a cost or by individuals who undertake to make good – up to the gross value of the estate – any deficiency caused by the administrators failing in their duties.

Letters of administration may also be taken out by creditors of an estate if executors deliberately do not apply for probate – for instance, if the estate has insufficient assets to pay all creditors and legatees.

The grant of probate

There may be a time lapse of six weeks or more between lodging the probate papers and the meeting at the registry to sign and swear them. After this has happened, however, things move quickly. If there is no inheritance tax to be paid – where the net estate is less than £325,000, or where the deceased property goes to the spouse – the grant of probate (or letters of administration) is issued within a few days. If inheritance tax is due, it takes two to three weeks before the exact amount is calculated and the grant is usually ready about a week later. The grant of probate is signed by an officer of the probate registry. Attached to the grant of probate is a photocopy of the will. (all original wills are kept at the Principal Probate Registry in London). Each page of your copy of the will carries the impress of the courts official seal. It is accompanied by a note which explains the procedure for collecting and distributing the estate and advises representatives to take legal advice in the event of dispute or other difficulty.

**

Chapter 5

Post Probate-The Distribution of the Estate

The distribution of the estate of the deceased

Having established probate, it is now time to begin to distribute the estate. Before you can do this, however, it is essential that you understand exactly what the will says. The executor can be sued for payment if the estate is not distributed exactly in accordance with the stipulations in the will. Although this may sound like common sense, some wills may be couched in a particular way, or in a particular jargon and you may need advice on the interpretation.

Specific legacies and bequests

Legacies are, usually, the payment of specific sums of money. Bequests usually mean gifts of goods or cash. 'Devises' means gifts of land or buildings. If the state is not subject to inheritance tax and the legacies and bequests are small, legacies can be paid without further delay and also specific items can be handed over. It is advisable to obtain a receipt from the beneficiary(s) when they receive their gift or legacy.

Transferring property

If a beneficiary has been left a house or other property then any outstanding debts relating to the property, such as a mortgage have to be dealt with. The will usually directs the executors to pay off the mortgage. However, if the will is silent on this point then it will become the responsibility of the beneficiary. It is quite usual that a property is left to another with a mortgage and equity in the property so the beneficiary can continue to pay.

Further, it is not necessary for a Personal Representative to transfer the property into their own name, before selling the property to a third party. Gov.uk provides guidance and a property can be directly assented to the beneficiaries using form AS1.

Preparation of final accounts

In appendix one, there are samples of letters which need to be sent having received the grant of representation. These letters are usually follow on letters from the pre-probate process where you are now claiming assets from banks, building societies, pension funds, employers, stockbrokers and so on. Having gathered the assets and obtained a good idea of the value you can now begin to prepare final accounts. There is no set form for

73

the final accounts but assets and liabilities must be included, receipts and payments made during the administration and a distribution account of payments to beneficiaries.

It is helpful to include a covering sheet to the accounts, a form of memorandum which will cover the following areas:

- Details of the deceased and date of death, date of probate and names of executors
- A summary of the bequests made in the will
- Particulars of property transfers
- Reference to any valuations which have been included in the accounts

In estates where inheritance tax has been paid, you should prepare one part of the capital account based on the value of the assets at the time of death.

The second part of the account should demonstrate the value of those assets and liabilities at the date they are realised or paid. If the net effect is to reduce the value of the estate, you may be able to claim a refund from the capital taxes office. Conversely you may have increased taxes to pay. In either case you should advise the capital taxes office.

A model set of accounts are shown at the end of the chapter. The capital account shows the value of assets when they are cashed or realised and the debts are the sums actually paid. The income account shows the income received during the administration, less associated expenses. It is convenient to run this account from the date of death to the following 5th of April.

The distribution account shows the capital and income transferred from the respective accounts and how the residue of the estate has been divided. If there is only one beneficiary you should show the final figure. If any items have been taken in kind – such as a car or a piece of furniture – its value is included in the distribution account as both an asset and payment. If you are claiming executor's expenses itemise them and include them in the distribution account.

Where a will exists

When you have completed your accounts, and all outstanding debts and liabilities have been met, you will now be in a position to calculate how much each residuary beneficiary receives

75

according to the specific provisions of the will. In practice, the amount that you have left in the executor's bank account should match the sums to be paid out.

After having ascertained that this is the case, and rectified any errors you should send the accounts to the beneficiaries for their agreement or otherwise. In cases involving inheritance tax, you should contact the capital taxes office and confirm that you have disclosed the full value of the estate. You then apply for a clearance certificate. When you have received this you can make the final distribution to the beneficiaries. The beneficiaries should be asked to sign an acknowledgement that they agree the accounts and that they agree the amount that they will receive.

Where beneficiaries are deceased or missing

If a beneficiary dies before the death of the testator, the general rule is that the legacy cannot be made. There are a few exceptions to this rule:

- If the will contains a 'substitution' (an alternative to the beneficiary)
- If the gift is made to two people as joint tenants – the survivor being the beneficiary

- If section 33(2) of the Wills Act 1837 applies. This section provides that, if the share of the estate or gift is to a child or other descendant of the testator and the child dies before the testator leaving 'issue' (children and their descendants) they take the share of the gift.

If a beneficiary cannot be located, you must take steps to find that person. These steps must be reasonable. As stated, an advertisement can suffice, as well as contacting relatives and so on. You can apply to the court for an order giving you permission to distribute the estate on agreed terms You can claim any expenses incurred from the estate. It is very important, if you cannot find a beneficiary that you take steps to obtain a court order in order to protect yourself from any future problems arising should a beneficiary turn up.

In some cases, intestacy rules can be rigid and cause hardship. You should always take advice when dealing with distribution of assets in cases that are complicated to resolve.

See overleaf for an example of administration accounts.

EXAMPLE OF ADMINISTRATION ACCOUNTS	
In the estate of (Deceased)	
Date of death	
Capital Account	
Assets	
House net sales proceeds Value at death £155, 000	£145,000
Less mortgage	£95,000
Total	**£50,000**
Stocks and Shares	£89,000
(value at death £86500)	
Life policy	£7500
Skipton BS deposit	£9000
Interest to date of death	£75
National Savings-Premium bonds	£7000
Arrears of pension	£325
Agreed value of house contents	£3800
Car	55600
Gross estate	**£172,300**
Less debts and liabilities	
Funeral costs	£2000
Gas	£270
Electricity	£25
Administration expenses	£45
Probate fees	£130
Stockbrokers valuation fee	£250
Income tax paid to date of death	£650

Net Estate carried to distribution account	**£168930**
For the estate to attract inheritance tax the value would need to be above £325,000. If that is the case, carry on the calculation for inheritance tax by multiplying the residue after £325,000 by 40% which will give you the inheritance tax due.	
In the estate of the deceased	
Income account (Column one)	**Net Dividend**
Holding company	
5,000 shares ABC Plc	£1400
4300 shares Halifax PLC	£560
12000 shares GKN	£1420
3760 shares Powergen	£420
Savings account (final interest)	£150
Balance transferred to distribution account	3950
In the estate of (deceased)	
Distribution account	
Balance transferred from capital account	£168930
balance transferred from income account	£3950
Less payment of legacies	

David Peters	£5,000
Net residuary for distribution	£167880
Mr Frederick Dillon	
A one half share represented by	
House contents	£3800
The balance	£80140
Stella Donaldson	
One half share represented by the balance	£83940
Total	**£167880**

****

Glossary of terms

Administrator-The person who administers the estate of a person who has died intestate

Bequest-A gift of a particular object or cash as opposed to 'devise' which means land or buildings

Chattels-Personal belongings of the deceased

Child-Referred to in a will or intestacy – child of the deceased including adopted and illegitimate children but, unless specifically included in a will, not stepchildren

Cohabitee-A partner of the deceased who may be able to claim a share of the estate. The term 'common law wife' has no legal force.

Confirmation-The document issued to executors by the sheriff court in Scotland to authorise them to administer the estate

Devise-A gift of house or land

Disposition-A formal conveyancing document in Scotland

Estate-All the assets and property of the deceased, including houses, cars, investments, money and personal belongings

Executor-The person appointed in the will to administer the estate of a deceased person

Heritable estate-Land and buildings in Scotland

Inheritance tax-The tax which may be payable when the total estate of the deceased person exceeds a set threshold (subject to various exemptions and adjustments)

Intestate-A person who dies without making a will

Issue-All the descendants of a person, i.e. children, grandchildren, great grandchildren#

Legacy-A gift of money

Minor-A person under 18 years of age

Moveable estate-Property other than land or buildings in Scotland

Next of Kin-The person entitled to the estate when a person dies intestate

Letters of administration-The document issued to administrators by a probate registry to authorise them to administer the estate of an intestate

Personal estate or personalty-All the investments and belongings of a person apart from land and buildings

Personal representatives-A general term for both administrators and executors

Probate of the will-The document issued to executors by a probate registry in England, Wales and Northern Ireland to authorise them to administer the estate

Probate Registry-The Government office which deals with probate maters. The principal Probate Registry is in London with district registries in cities and some large towns

Real estate or realty-Land and buildings owned by a person

Residue-What is left of the estate to share out after all the debts and specific bequests and legacies have been paid

Specific bequests-Particular items gifted by will

Testator--A person who makes a will

Will-The document in which you say what is to happen to your estate after death

**

Useful Addresses and Websites

Department for National Savings

Glasgow G58 1SB

For enquiries about Capital Bonds, Childrens Bonus Bonds, FIRST Option Bonds, Fixed Rate Savings Bonds, Ordinary Accounts and Investment Accounts.

www.nsandi.com

Tel: 08085 007 007

Department for Work and Pensions

Caxton House

Tothill Street

London

SW1H 9NA

https://www.gov.uk/government/organisations/department-for-work-pensions

HM Revenue and Customs Capital Taxes Office

Tel: 0300 123 1072

The Law Society of England and Wales

www.lawsociety.org.uk

London Gazette

London

The London Gazette

PO Box 3584

Norwich NR7 7WD

T: +44 (0)333 200 2434

F: +44 (0)333 202 5080

E: london@thegazette.co.uk

Edinburgh

The Edinburgh Gazette

PO Box 3584

Norwich NR7 7WD

T: +44 (0)333 200 2434

F: +44 (0)333 202 5080

E: edinburgh@thegazette.co.uk

Belfast

The Belfast Gazette

TSO Ireland

19a Weavers Court, Weavers Court Business Park

Linfield Road

Belfast BT12 5GH

T: +44 (0)28 9089 5135

F: +44 (0)28 9023 5401

E: belfast@thegazette.co.uk

Solicitors Regulation Authority

The Cube

199 Wharfside Street

Birmingham B1 1RN

www.sra.org.uk

0370 606 2555

Information on solicitors specialising in wills and probate

The Principal Probate Registry

First Avenue House

42-49 High Holborn

London WC1V 6NP

Probate Helpline 0300 123 1072

Useful Addresses in Scotland

Accountant of Court

Scottish Courts and Tribunals Service

Saughton House

Broomhouse Drive

Edinburgh

EH11 3XD

Tel 0131 444 3300

Fax 0131 443 2610

enquiries@scotcourts.gov.uk

Law Society of Scotland

Atria One

144 Morrison Street

Edinburgh

EH3 8EX

0131 226 7411

www.lawscot.org.uk

Registers of Scotland

0800 169 9391

(Head Office)

ros.gov.uk

Sheriff Clerks Office

Commissary Department

27 Chambers Street

Edinburgh EH1 1LB-0131 225 2525

Appendix 1

Example letters

Sample letter which should accompany the advertisement for creditors and claimants-local newspaper

The   Daily Times

Dear Sirs/Madam

In respect of   Deceased

Further to our discussions, please find enclosed an advertisement pursuant to Section 27 of the Trustee Act 1925. Please insert this into your newspaper for one week only.

Yours faithfully

Letter to the London Gazette requesting form for advertising for claimants and creditors.

To: The Manager

the London Gazette

PO Box 7923

London SE1 5ZH

Dear Sir/Madam

Could you please send me a form for completion to enable me to have an advertisement placed in the London Gazette pursuant to section 27 of the Trustees Act 1925. Please let me have a note of any fees payable to you.

Yours faithfully

To The London Gazette enclosing a form for advertisement for claimants and creditors

To: The Manager

the London Gazette

PO Box 7923

London SE1 5ZH

Dear Sir/Madam

Re: The Deceased

Please find enclosed an advertisement for claimants and creditors plus office copy of grant of representation for inspection and return, along with a cheque for payment. Please publish the advertisement in the first available issue of the Gazette.

Yours faithfully

Letters to be sent pre-grant of probate

Letters to banks and building societies

The manager

(Bank/Building Society)

Dear Sir/Madam

I am the executor/administrator of the estate of your customer (insert name and address plus account numbers as appropriate). This person passed away on the   and I enclose a registrar's death certificate and a copy of the will (if there is a will).

Please could you let me have any details of accounts, all accounts, which the deceased has with your organisation, particulars of any assets or securities held for safe custody plus any other financial documents which will be relevant in forming a picture of the estate.

Please forward the following in respect of each account held in the deceased's name:

1. balance of account as at the date of death plus any interest owed.

2. Interest accrued to the account between the end of the last

financial year and the date of death.

3. Whether the interest is paid gross or net.

4. Whether there are any direct debits or standing orders in respect of each account. please supply particulars.

Any other credit balances on non-interest bearing accounts in the deceased's sole name should be placed on deposit until production of the grant of probate has been given.

Can you let me know your requirements for closing the accounts in the deceased's sole name, and let me have any necessary forms. Please confirm that any accounts held jointly can continue to be operated by the surviving account holder.

Please cancel any standing orders in respect of the accounts and do not meet any further direct debits.

Please send all future communications to me at the above address. please do not hesitate to contact me on the above phone number.

Please find enclosed (passbooks etc).

Yours faithfully

Letter to registrars of companies in respect of stocks and shares

To: The Registrar (Company name address)

Dear Sir/madam

Re: (Deceased) (Company name and share account number etc)

I am the personal representative of   and I enclose a death certificate for your attention. Please register and return.

Can you please confirm the extent of the deceased's holding and let me have the transfer deeds for completion to enable the transfer to beneficiaries when probate is obtained.

Yours faithfully

Letter to Stockbrokers

To: (Company name address)

Dear Sir/madam

I am the personal representative of   and I enclose a death certificate for your attention. Please register and return.

Please let me have a statement of the deceased nominee account with you as at the date of death specifying the deceased holdings and cash position. This is for the purposes of distribution on obtaining probate.

Yours faithfully

Letter to creditors

To: (Insert name and address of creditor)

Dear Sir/Madam

Re: Account number

I am the executor/proposed administrator of the estate of who died on and I enclose a death certificate for your records. Please return original.

Please let me have a final statement detailing the amount claimed. Please note, in light of the fact that the debtor has died, please take no enforcement action until the estate is in funds, probate is granted and distributions made.

All future correspondence re the deceased should be sent to the above address.

Yours faithfully

Letter to employer

To (employer)

Attention of the payroll department

Deaf Sir/Madam

Re: (Deceased) (Payroll number if known)

I am the executor/administrator of the above estate who died on
and who was employed by your company as
I enclose a death certificate for your records please return the original.

Please supply the following:

1. Whether any salary is due to the above and your requirements for them to be claimed.

2. The gross amount of salary paid in the current financial year and income tax paid.

3. Whether the above was a member of a pension fund. if so, please supply details.

4. The name and address of the tax district relevant to the deceased.

All future communications should be sent to me at the above address.

Yours faithfully

Letter to HMRC in respect of Income tax

To HM Inspector of Taxes

(Name and Address)

Insert tax reference if known

Dear Sir/Madam

I am the executor/administrator of the estate of (Deceased) who died on   I enclose a death certificate for your records. please copy and return the original.

Please supply me with a copy of the deceased's last tax return and the appropriate forms to enable me to make a return to the date of death and in due course a personal representative's return for the period to the finalisation of the estate.

Please let me have details of any tax outstanding or any repayments due to the deceased and your requirements to enable these matters to be dealt with.

Please address all future communications to me at the above address.

Yours faithfully

Letter to mortgage company

To: The Manager (name and address of company)

Dear Sir/madam

(Mortgage reference address of property mortgaged and name of deceased)

I am the executor/administrator of the above named customer who died on   I enclose a death certificate for you to copy and return the original.

Can you please let me know the capital amount outstanding on the account to the date of death. Please also let me know the amount of interest outstanding at the date of death.

Please let me have details of any endowment policy and the company involved. The grant of representation will be registered with you when it has been granted and I will then let you know the position concerning the mortgage, i.e. whether it is to be paid off or continued in the beneficiaries name.

Until that time, please see that no enforcement action be taken. Please send all correspondence to the above address.

Yours faithfully

Letter to pension fund where pension is already being paid

To: The Secretary

(Name and address)

Dear Sir/madam

Insert details of pension number name etc

I am the executor/administrator of the estate of   who

died on   I enclose a death certificate which should be copied with the original returned.

   Please let me know:

1. Whether there are any arrears of pension due to the estate to the date of death or any overpaid pension due to be refunded to the pension fund.

2. Your requirements to enable you to pay any arrears.

3. the gross amount of pension payable in the current tax year, including sums to the date of death but not yet paid.

4. the amount of tax deducted or which will be deducted from the current tax years pension.

5. the address and reference number for the relevant tax district.

All communications re the above should now be addressed to me.

Yours faithfully

To pension fund where pension is not yet being paid

The Secretary

(name and address)

Dear Sir/madam

Re: (Deceased) (pension number)

I am the executor/administrator of the estate of   who is a contributor to a pension fund administered by you. The deceased passed away on   and I enclose a death certificate for your records. please return the original.

I understand that the deceased, who was employed by   was a member of your scheme. Please let me know what benefits are due to the deceased's estate and dependants and whether the benefits are subject to inheritance tax. Please send all correspondence concerning the deceased to the above address.

Yours faithfully

Letters Post-Grant of Representation
Banks and building societies

To: The Manager

Address

Dear Sir/madam

Name and account number

Further to my recent correspondence to you, please find an office copy grant of probate/letters of administration for your records. please note and return.

I enclose the completed withdrawal forms for your attention.

Please close the account and let me have a remittance for the sum due together with a final statement of account.

Yours faithfully

To registrars in respect of shares and stock (certificated holdings)

To: the registrar

Name and address

Dear Sir/madam

Re: Deceased name and address reference number

I am the personal representative of   and I enclose an office copy of grant of representation for your records and to return. I also enclose the relevant certificates together with the un-cashed (dividend/interest) warrant(s) in respect of the holdings set out below.

Please amend or reissue the warrants in my name so that they can be paid into the estates bank account. Please endorse the certificates so that they can be sold.

Yours faithfully

Stock brokers

To

name and address

Dear Sirs

Re: (name and reference number if known)

I am the personal representative of   and I enclose an office copy of grant of representation for registration and return in respect of the deceased's holdings in (name of relevant companies)

Please transfer/sell the holdings as follows (set out details of the required transfers or sales for each company stating the relevant number of shares or amount of stock, and name and address of each transferee if transfers are required).

Yours faithfully

Creditors paying account

To

Name and address

Dear Sirs

Re: My previous communication in respect of

I enclose a cheque in the sum of   in settlement of your enclosed account. Please send a receipt as soon as possible.

Yours faithfully

Inspector of taxes notifying end of administration period and enclosing final tax return

> To: HM Inspector of Taxes
>
> Name and address
>
> tax reference
>
> Dear Sir/madam
> Re: (Deceased details)
>
> No further income is anticipated in respect of the above estate. Accordingly, please find enclosed the final tax return in respect of the estate, together with the certificates of deduction of tax from your income. Please return the certificates to me in due course.
>
> Please let me have a final tax assessment in respect of the estate.
>
> I shall be obliged if you will also let me have (number required) forms R185E in respect of the beneficiaries.
> Yours faithfully

Letter to capital tax office requesting inheritance tax clearance.

To: Capital taxes

Farrers House

PO Box 38

Castle Meadow Road

Nottingham

NG2 1BB

Dear Sir/Madam

Re: (Capital taxes reference, deceased details)

I would be grateful if you would let me have a formal inheritance tax clearance at your earliest convenience.

Yours faithfully

Letter to residuary beneficiaries enclosing accounts for approval

To: (name and address of beneficiary)

Dear

Re: the estate of (deceased)

The administration of the estate of the above has now been completed and I enclose copies of accounts in duplicate for your approval. Accounts have also been sent to the other parties fro their approval.

If you approve the accounts, please sign and date the form of discharge at the bottom of one copy and return that copy to me.

When all parties have returned the accounts to me approved I will be in a position to let you have a remittance for monies due to you.

If you have any queries please do not hesitate to contact me.

Yours faithfully

Intestacy Rules from 1st October 2014

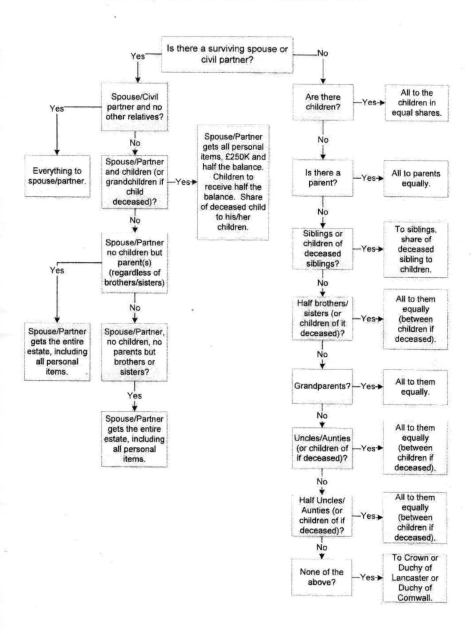

Appendix 3 – Example forms to be used in the process of probate

1. N205D Notice of issue of a Probate claim.

2. PA1A-Died without a Will

3. PA1P-Died with a will

4. PA2 How to obtain probate without a solicitor

5. PA3 Probate fees

The above five forms are shown in appendix 1

For all other forms connected with the probate process go to:

www.gov.uk/government/collections/probate-forms

otice of issue
robate claim)

In the

Claim No.

Claimant(s)

Defendant(s)

Issue fee

the estate of   deceased (Probate)

ur claim was issued on [   ]

ne court sent it to the defendant(s) by first class post on [   ]
d it will be deemed served on [   ]].

ne claim form (which includes particulars of claim) is returned to you, with the relevant response forms, for
ı to serve them on the defendant(s)]

tes for guidance
e claim form and particulars of claim, if served separately, must be served on the defendant within 4 months
the date of issue (6 months if you are serving outside England and Wales). You may be able to apply to
end the time for serving the claim form but the application must generally be made before the 4 month or
nonth period expires.

ıu must inform the court immediately if your claim is settled.

e defendant must file an acknowledgment of service and defence within 28 days of service of the Particulars
Claim (whether they are served with the claim form or separately). A longer period applies if the defendant
served outside England and Wales.

fault judgment **cannot** be obtained in a probate claim.

ıo defendant acknowledges service or files a defence, and the time for doing so has expired, you may apply to
court for an order that the claim proceed to trial.

To

Ref.

PA1A — Probate application

This form is for an application where the person who has died **did not leave a will** that deals with assets in England and Wales

Checklist – before you send your application form to HMCTS Probate you will need to enclose the following. This checklist must be completed. If you do not enclose all of the required documents it will delay your application. Please keep copies of all documents that you send.

Did you know you can apply for Probate online?

Go to www.gov.uk/wills-probate-inheritance/appyling-for-a-grant-of-representation

- [ ] PA1A - Probate Application (this form)
- [ ] Inheritance Tax Summary Form: Please submit the appropriate form (IHT205 or IHT207, and IHT217 if applicable), signed by all applicants (see additional notes in Section 6).
- [ ] A copy of any foreign wills or any wills dealing with assets held outside England and Wales (and if not in English, an English translation).
- [ ] An official copy (**not** a photocopy) of the death certificate, or a coroner's interim certificate of the person who has died.
- [ ] Any other documents requested on this form. Please list them:

As well as the application fee, there is a fee for each official copy of the Grant of Representation that we provide.

How many official copies of the Grant of Representation do you require for use **in** the United Kingdom?

How many official copies of the Grant of Representation do you require for use **outside** of the United Kingdom?

Application fee	£
Fees for copies	£
Total fees	£

- [ ] Debit or Credit card. (This payment must be made before you send your application and the payment reference entered in the box below.)

Payment reference

- [ ] A cheque/postal order payable to '**HMCTS**' in respect of HMCTS's fees. Please write the name of the person who has died on the back of the cheque.

Details of how to pay by debit or credit card can be found at www.gov.uk/wills-probate-inheritance/applying-for-a-grant-of-representation

Please see leaflet PA4SOT for where to make your payment and send your application forms. This can be downloaded from hmctsformfinder.justice.gov.uk

About the applicant(s) – All applicants must be over 18 years and a maximum of 4 may apply

1 Title and full name including middle names of **first applicant**

Title

First name(s)

Middle name(s)

Last name

2 Your address

Building and street

Second line of address

Town or city

County (optional)

Postcode

1.3   Your home telephone number

[ ][ ][ ][ ][ ][ ][ ][ ][ ][ ][ ][ ][ ][ ]

1.4   Your mobile/work telephone number

[ ][ ][ ][ ][ ][ ][ ][ ][ ][ ][ ][ ][ ][ ]

1.5   Your email address

[ ][ ][ ][ ][ ][ ][ ][ ][ ][ ][ ][ ][ ][ ][ ][ ][ ]

[ ][ ][ ][ ][ ][ ][ ][ ][ ][ ][ ][ ][ ][ ][ ][ ][ ]

Note 1.5 – we will contact you with any queries via this email address.
We aim to contact you within 10 working days of receipt of your application.

1.6   Title and full name including middle names of **second applicant**

Title

[ ][ ][ ][ ][ ][ ][ ][ ][ ]

First name(s)

[ ][ ][ ][ ][ ][ ][ ][ ][ ][ ][ ][ ][ ][ ][ ][ ][ ]

[ ][ ][ ][ ][ ][ ][ ][ ][ ][ ][ ][ ][ ][ ][ ][ ][ ]

Middle name(s)

[ ][ ][ ][ ][ ][ ][ ][ ][ ][ ][ ][ ][ ][ ][ ][ ][ ]

[ ][ ][ ][ ][ ][ ][ ][ ][ ][ ][ ][ ][ ][ ][ ][ ][ ]

Last name

[ ][ ][ ][ ][ ][ ][ ][ ][ ][ ][ ][ ][ ][ ][ ][ ][ ]

[ ][ ][ ][ ][ ][ ][ ][ ][ ][ ][ ][ ][ ][ ][ ][ ][ ]

7 Their address

Building and street

[   ]

Second line of address

[   ]

Town or city

[   ]

County (optional)

[   ]

Postcode

[| | | | | |]

8 Their email address

[   ]

[   ]

9 Title and full name including middle names of **third applicant**

Title

[   ]

First name(s)

[   ]

[   ]

Middle name(s)

[   ]

[   ]

Last name

[   ]

[   ]

1.10 Their address

Building and street

Second line of address

Town or city

County (optional)

Postcode

1.11 Their email address

1.12 Title and full name including middle names of **fourth applicant**

Title

First name(s)

Middle name(s)

Last name

13 Their address

Building and street

Second line of address

Town or city

County (optional)

Postcode

14 Their email address

SECTION B

The information you provide in this section of the application form will be the basis of your statement of truth, and it will be stored as a public record.

If you need help filling out this form please call the

**Probate Helpline
0300 123 1072**

We cannot provide legal advice

2. About the person who has died

2.1 Forename(s) (including all middle names) as they appear on the Death Certificate

2.2 Surname as it appears on the Death Certificate

2.3 Permanent address

Building and street

Second line of address

Town or city

County (optional)

Postcode

2.4 Date they were born

2.5 Date they died

2.6 Was the person who has died known by any other name in which they held assets?

☐ Yes, **go to question 2.7**

☐ No, **go to question 2.8**

7 Please give the details of any other names by which the person who has died held assets.

Full name

Note 2.7 – These names must be ones that will appear on the grant because an asset is in that name. We do not need to know the asset.

8 Did the person who died live permanently in England and Wales at the date of death, or intend to return to England and Wales to live permanently? (For legal purposes this generally means they were domiciled in England and Wales. You may wish to seek legal advice about this.)

☐ Yes

☐ No

Note 2.8 – Living permanently means they had either their permanent or principal home in England and Wales at the date of death or they intended to return to England and Wales to live permanently.

9 Was the person who has died or any of their relatives legally adopted in or out of the family?

☐ Yes, see note 2.9

☐ No, **go to question 2.11**

Note 2.9 – If you answered Yes to this question we may require additional information to be submitted once we have received your application.

10 Please name the legally adopted relatives and give their relationship to the person who has died. Please state whether they were adopted into the family of the person who has died, or 'adopted out' (become part of someone else's family).

Name	Relationship	Adopted in or out

2.11 What was the marital status of the person who has died when they died?

☐ Never married

☐ Widowed, their lawful spouse or civil partner having died before them

☐ Married/in a civil partnership - give date

☐ Divorced/civil partnership is dissolved - give date

☐ Judicially separated - give date

2.12 What is the name of the court where the Decree Absolute, Decree of Dissolution of Partnership or Decree of Judicial Separation was issued?

2.13 Did the person who has died own any foreign assets?

☐ Yes, the total value of their foreign assets (not including houses or land)

£

☐ No

2.14 Was there any land vested in the person who has died which was settled previously to their death and which remained settled land not withstanding their death?

☐ Yes

☐ No

Note 2.11 – a civil partnership i a same-sex relationship that has been registered in accordance with the Civil Partnership Act 2004. A marriage is a legal ceremony conducted in UK under the Marriage Acts 1949, 1994 and The Marriage (Same Sex Marriage) Act 2013 or unde legislation in any other country by the law applicable there. Date of divorce - this date is on their Decree Absolute, Decree of Dissolution of Partnership or Decree of Judicial Separation. You can get an official copy of these documents from the court that issued them, or from The Divorce Absolute Search Section, Central Family Court, 42–49 High Holborn, London WC1V 6NP.

Note 2.14 – It is rare for estates to be subject to the provisions of the Settled Land Act 1925 but if you know this applies or have any queries please seek legal advice.

Relatives of the person who has died

1 Did the person who has died leave a surviving lawful spouse or civil partner?

☐ Yes

☐ No

Note 3.1 – 'survive' means that they were alive when the deceased person died.

2 How many of the following blood and adoptive relatives did the person who has died have?

	Under 18 years	Over 18 years
a How many sons or daughters of the person who died survived them?		
b How many sons or daughters of the person who has died who did not survive them?		
c How many children of people at 'b' who survived them?		

Note 3.2 – Please state the **number** of relatives the person who has died had in the relevant sections. If none then put nil or strike through. If you are unsure about the relationships of the persons applying then contact HMCTS Probate.

Please confirm that if any of the applicants are grandchildren of the deceased (3.2c) that their parent is one of the persons referred to at 3.2b. If they are not then they are not able to apply.

☐ Yes

If you have entered details in any of the boxes above go to Q3.5. If not then proceed to question 3.3

Note – Depending on the value of the net estate the lawful spouse/civil partner may not be the only person entitled to the estate of the deceased. Please seek legal advice regarding the distribution of the estate.

All relatives from the same category as the applicant are entitled to share in the estate including children/issue of any who have predeceased. You should seek legal advice regarding distribution of the estate if you are in any doubt.

3.3 How many of the following blood and adoptive relatives did the person who has died have?

If you have filled in details in any of the sections in question 3.2, then go to question 3.5

		Under 18 years	Over 18 years
d	How many parents of the person who has died survived them?		
e	How many Whole-blood brothers or sisters of the person who has died survived them?		
f	How many Whole-blood brothers or sisters of the person who has died did not survive them?		
g	How many Children of people at section (f) survived them?		
h	How many Half-blood brothers or sisters of the person who has died survived them?		
i	How many Half-blood brothers or sisters of the person who has died did not survive them?		
j	How many Children of people at section (i) survived them?		

Please confirm that if any of the applicants are nephews or neices of the whole or half blood of the deceased (questions 3.3g and 3.3j) that their parent is one of the persons referred to at 3.3f or 3.3i. If they are not then they are not able to apply.

☐ Yes

If you have entered details in any of the boxes above go to Q3.5. If not then go to question 3.4.

Note 3.3 – Once you have entered a number in one of the block sections (e.g. d to j) you should go to question 3.5

Step-relatives should not be included.

A '**whole-blood**' brother or sister is someone who has both parents in common with person who has died, or someone who was legally adopted by both of the parents of the person who has died.

A '**half-blood**' brother or sister is someone who has only one parent in common with the person who has died or someone who was legally adopted by only one of the parents of the person who has died.

4 How many of the following blood and adoptive relatives did the person who has died have?

If you have filled in details in any of the sections in question 3.3, then go to question 3.5.

		Under 18 years	Over 18 years
a	How many Grandparents of the person who has died survived them?		
b	How many Whole-blood uncles or aunts of the person who has died survived them?		
c	How many Whole-blood uncles or aunts of the person who has died did not survive them?		
d	How many Children of people at 3.4c who survived them?		
e	How many Half-blood uncles or aunts of the person who has died survived them?		
f	How many Half-blood uncles or aunts of the person who has died did not survived them?		
g	How many Children of people at 3.4f who survived them?		

Note 3.4 – this section should only be completed if no relatives have been entered in section 3.3. Please state the number of relatives the person who has died had in the relevant sections. If none then put nil or strike through.

Step-relatives and people who were related to the person who has died only by marriage should not be included.

A '**whole-blood**' uncle or aunt is someone who has both parents in common with the mother or father of the person who has died, or someone who was legally adopted by the maternal or paternal grandparents of the person who has died.

A '**half-blood**' uncle or aunt is someone who has only one parent in common with the mother or father of the person who has died or someone who was legally adopted by only one of the grandparents of the person who has died.

Please confirm that if any of the applicants are cousins of the whole or half blood of the deceased (questions 3.4d and 3.4g) and that their parent is one of the persons referred to at 3.4c or 3.4f. If they are not then they are not able to apply.

☐ Yes

5. Please state the relationship of each of the persons applying for the grant to the person who has died. (If you are applying as an attorney for someone then please state attorney)

Relationship description

First applicant

Second applicant

Third applicant

Fourth applicant

4. Applying as an attorney

4.1 Are you applying as an attorney on behalf of one or more people who are entitled to apply for a Grant of Representation? **Please read Note 4 before proceeding.**

☐ Yes, **go to question 4.2**

☐ No, **go to section 5**

4.2 Please give the full names of the person or people on whose behalf you are applying and their relationship to the person who has died.

4.3 Please give their address

Building and street

Second line of address

Town or city

County (optional)

Postcode

4.4 Is a person on whose behalf you are applying unable to make a decision for themselves due to an impairment of or a disturbance in the functioning of their mind or brain?

☐ Yes, further confirmation of this will be requested by the Probate Registry.

☐ No

4.5 Has anyone been appointed by the Court of Protection to act on behalf of a person on whose behalf you are applying including the right to apply for a grant of representation?

☐ Yes, **please provide an official copy of the court order with your application**

☐ No

Note 4 – if you are applying on behalf of more than one person, please provide the information requested in this section for the other people you represent on a separate sheet of paper. We will need to send you a further form for the person who is appointing you as their attorney to sign.

Please visit GOV.UK (gov.uk/wills-probate-inheritance/if-youre-an-executor) to print off the PA12 attorney form or call 0117 9302430 and quote 'Attorney' and we will send the attorney form.

You will need to send the attorney form to us with this application.

Where there are persons aged under 18 benefiting from the estate then two applicants (or at least two) will be needed in Section A. You may wish to contact HMCTS Probate to seek information in regard to who is eligible to apply.

Note 4.4 – this applies if they lack capacity under the Mental Capacity Act 2005 and are incapable of managing their property and financial affairs. You may wish to seek legal advice about this.

In some cases you may be asked to provide medical evidence. If you do not already have medical evidence from a qualified practitioner or are using a registered LPA a short form of medical evidence will be required.

Please visit GOV.UK (gov.uk/wills-probate-inheritance/if-youre-an-executor) to print off the PA14 medical certifgicate or call 0117 9302430 and quote 'medical evidence' and we will send the form.

6   Has a person on whose behalf you are applying appointed an attorney under an Enduring Power of Attorney (EPA) or a Property and Financial Affairs Lasting Power of Attorney (LPA)?

☐ Yes, **please provide the original EPA/LPA (or a solicitor's certified copy of it certified on every page.) with your application**

☐ No, **go to Section 6**

Note 4.6 – an LPA must be registered with the Office of the Public Guardian before it can be used.

7   Has the Enduring Power of Attorney (EPA) been registered with the Office of the Public Guardian?

☐ Yes

☐ No

5. Foreign domicile

**Note – if you answered Yes, to question 2.8 you don't need to complete this
section – please go to Section 6.**

5.1 What was the country where the person who died either lived permanently
at the date of death or intended to return to live permanently?

5.2 What does the estate in England and Wales of the person who has died
consist of?

Assets	Values

5.3 Has an entrusting document been issued by the court where the person who
has died was domiciled?

☐ Yes, **please provide the official document with your application; if it is
not in English, please also provide an official translation.
Go to Section 6.**

☐ No

5.4 Has a succession certificate, inheritance certificate or equivalent document
been issued by a court or Notary in the country of domicile of the person
who has died?

☐ Yes, **please provide the official document with your application; if it is
not in English, please also provide an official translation.**

☐ No

Note 5.3 and 5.4 – these
documents may help to
support your application.
If you do not have any of
these documents, you may
wish to seek legal advice.

Inheritance tax

1 Did you complete an Inheritance Tax Estate report online?

☐ Yes, do not submit an Inheritance Tax form with this application

Please provide the following details, **then go to Legal Statement**:

IHT Identifier [ ]

Gross Estate Figure £ [ ]

Net Estate Figure £ [ ]

☐ No, **go to question 6.2**

Note 6 – if you completed an Inheritance Tax Summary online, and fully complete question 6.1 of this form, you do not need to send an Inheritance Tax Estate report form with your application.

For guidance on probate fees please visit www. gov.uk/wills-probate-inheritance/

2 Which of the following inheritance tax forms have you completed?

☐ Form **IHT205**, **complete 6.3 then go to Legal Statement**

☐ Form **IHT207**, **complete 6.4 then go to Legal Statement**

☐ Forms **IHT400** and **IHT421**, **complete 6.5 then go to Legal Statement**

Note 6.2 – if you did not complete an Inheritance Tax Estate report online, you **must** complete IHT205, or IHT207, or both IHT400 and IHT421.

3 Provide the following figures from form **IHT205**.

Figure from box D £ [ ]

Figure from box F £ [ ]
(This figure will determine the probate application fee)

Note 6.3 – if the person who has died, died before 1 September 2006, it may affect which tax form you need to complete, so please ring the **Probate Helpline** on **0300 123 1072**.

4 Provide the following figures from form **IHT207**.

Figure from box A £ [ ]

Figure from box H £ [ ]
(This figure will determine the probate application fee)

5 Provide the following figures from form **IHT421**.

Figure from box 3 £ [ ]
(Gross value of assets)

Figure from box 5 £ [ ]
(Net value)
(This figure will determine the probate application fee)

Note 6.5 – do **not** send form IHT400 or form IHT421 to us. Please send them to HM Revenue and Customs, Inheritance Tax, BX9 1HT, at the same time you send PA1A and other papers to HMCTS Probate. HMRC will stamp your IHT421 and send it to HMCTS Probate.

LEGAL STATEMENT

The undersigned confirms:

- to collect the whole estate
- to keep full details (an inventory) of the estate
- to keep a full account of how the estate has been distributed

If the Probate Registry (court) asks the undersigned they will:

- Provide the full details of the estate and how it has been distributed
- Return the grant of representation to the court

and understand that:

- The application will be rejected if the information is not provided (if asked)
- Criminal proceedings for fraud may be brought against the undersigned if it is found that the evidence provided is deliberately untruthful or dishonest

The undersigned confirm to administer the estate of the person who has died in accordance to law, and that the application is truthful.

PLEASE MAKE SURE THAT ALL PERSONS APPLYING FOR THE GRANT SIGN THE DECLARATION BELOW.

Name of **first applicant**

Signature

Date signed

Name of **second applicant**

Signature

Date signed

Name of **third applicant**

Signature

Date signed

Name of **fourth applicant**

Signature

Date signed

Please see leaflet PA4SOT for where to make your payment and send your completed form.

Phone 0300 303 0648
Email contactprobate@justice.gov.uk

How are the applicants entitled to apply.

In what capacity are the persons applying entitled to apply?

☐ The undersigned is the wife or husband or civil partner of the person who
has died

☐ The undersigned is or are the child/children of the person who has died

☐ The undersigned is or are the grandchild/grandchildren of the person
who has died being the son or daughter of a child who died in the
lifetime of the person who has died.

☐ The undersigned is or are the parent/parents of the person who has died

☐ The undersigned is or are the brother(s) or sister (s) of of the whole/half
blood of the person who has died

☐ The undersigned is or are the niece/nephew (s) of the whole/half blood of
the person who has died being the son or daughter of a brother or sister
of the person who has died who died in their lifetime.

☐ Other (Please state in the box below the reason they are applying)

PA1P — Probate application

This form is for an application where the person who has died left a will

Checklist – before you send your application form to HMCTS Probate you will need to enclose the following. This checklist must be completed. If you do not enclose all of the required documents it will delay your application. Please keep copies of all documents that you send.

- [ ] PA1P - Probate Application (this form) - where a person who has died has left a will.
- [ ] Inheritance Tax Summary Form: Please submit the appropriate form (IHT205 or IHT207, and IHT217 if applicable), signed by all applicants (see additional notes in Section 7).
- [ ] The last original will and any codicils made since that will.
- [ ] A copy of any foreign wills or any wills dealing with assets held outside England and Wales (and if not in English, an English translation).
- [ ] An official copy (**not** a photocopy) of the death certificate, or a coroner's interim certificate of the person who has died.
- [ ] Any other documents requested on this form. Please list them:

As well as the application fee, there is a fee for each official copy of the Grant of Representation that we provide.

How many official copies of the Grant of Representation do you require for use **in** the United Kingdom?

How many official copies of the Grant of Representation do you require for use **outside** of the United Kingdom?

Application fee	£
Fees for copies	£
Total fees	£

- [ ] Debit or Credit card. (This payment must be made before you send your application and the payment reference entered in the box below.)

Payment reference

- [ ] A cheque/postal order payable to '**HMCTS**' in respect of HMCTS's fees. Please write the name of the person who has died on the back of the cheque.

Did you know you can apply for Probate online?

Go to www.gov.uk/wills-probate-inheritance/appyling-for-a-grant-of-representation

Checklist note – Do not attach anything to or remove anything from the original will/codicils. Also, make sure that you keep a copy for yourself.

Details of how to pay by debit or credit card can be found at www.gov.uk/wills-probate-inheritance/applying-for-a-grant-of-representation

Please see leaflet PA4SOT for where to make your payment and send your application forms. This can be downloaded from hmctsformfinder.justice.gov.uk

ECTION A – PERSONAL INFORMATION

Please complete in BLOCK capitals placing a tick in boxes where applicable.

About the applicant(s) – All applicants must be over 18 years and a maximum of 4 may apply

.1 Title and full name including middle names of **first applicant**

Title

☐☐☐☐☐☐☐☐

First name(s)

☐☐☐☐☐☐☐☐☐☐☐☐☐☐☐

☐☐☐☐☐☐☐☐☐☐☐☐☐☐☐

Middle name(s)

☐☐☐☐☐☐☐☐☐☐☐☐☐☐☐

☐☐☐☐☐☐☐☐☐☐☐☐☐☐☐

Last name

☐☐☐☐☐☐☐☐☐☐☐☐☐☐☐

☐☐☐☐☐☐☐☐☐☐☐☐☐☐☐

Note 1.1 –
all correspondence, including the Grant of Representation, will be sent to the first applicant named in this section.

Only list applicants who wish to be named on the grant in this section and they will be required to sign this document. Please note that the names you provide here must match the names provided on your formal ID. E.g. passport or Driving licence.

When there are no executors applying and there are persons aged under 18 benefiting from the estate then two applicants (or at least two) will be needed in Section A. You may wish to contact HMCTS Probate to seek information in regard to who is eligible to apply.

.2 Is your name different in the will and codicil?

☐ Yes, give the name as it appears in the will or codicil in the box below

☐ No

1.3 Your address

Building and street

Second line of address

Town or city

County (optional)

Postcode

1.4 Your home telephone number

1.5 Your mobile/work telephone number

1.6 Your email address

Note 1.6 – we will contact you with any queries via this email address.
We aim to contact you within 10 working days of receipt of your application.

7 Title and full name including middle names of **second applicant**

Title

☐☐☐☐☐☐☐☐

First name(s)

☐☐☐☐☐☐☐☐☐☐☐☐☐☐☐☐☐☐

☐☐☐☐☐☐☐☐☐☐☐☐☐☐☐☐☐☐

Middle name(s)

☐☐☐☐☐☐☐☐☐☐☐☐☐☐☐☐☐☐

☐☐☐☐☐☐☐☐☐☐☐☐☐☐☐☐☐☐

Last name

☐☐☐☐☐☐☐☐☐☐☐☐☐☐☐☐☐☐

☐☐☐☐☐☐☐☐☐☐☐☐☐☐☐☐☐☐

8 Is their name different in the will and codicil?

☐ Yes, give the name as it appears in the will or codicil in the box below

☐ No

9 Their address

Building and street

Second line of address

Town or city

County (optional)

Postcode

☐☐☐☐☐☐☐

4

1.10 Their email address

1.11 Title and full name including middle names of **third applicant**

Title

First name(s)

Middle name(s)

Last name

1.12 Is their name different in the will and codicil?

☐ Yes, give the name as it appears in the will or codicil in the box below

☐ No

13 Their address

Building and street

Second line of address

Town or city

County (optional)

Postcode

14 Their email address

15 Title and full name including middle names of **fourth applicant**

Title

First name(s)

Middle name(s)

Last name

1.16 Is their name different in the will and codicil?

☐ Yes, give the name as it appears in the will or codicil in the box below

[ ]

☐ No

1.17 Their address

Building and street

[ ]

Second line of address

[ ]

Town or city

[ ]

County (optional)

[ ]

Postcode

[ ]

1.18 Their email address

[ ]

[ ]

SECTION B

The information you provide in this section of the application form will be the basis of your statement of truth, and it will be stored as a public record.

2. About the person who has died

2.1 Forename(s) (including all middle names) as they appear on the Death Certificate

2.2 Surname as it appears on the Death Certificate

2.3 Permanent address

Building and street

Second line of address

Town or city

County (optional)

Postcode

2.4 Date they were born

2.5 Date they died

2.6 Was the person who has died known by any other name in which they held assets?

☐ Yes, **go to question 2.7**

☐ No, **go to question 2.8**

2.7 Please give the details of any other names by which the person who has died held assets.

Full name

Note 2.7 – These names must be ones that will appear on the grant because an asset is in that name. We do not need to know the asset.

2.8 Did the person who died live permanently in England and Wales at the date of death, or intend to return to England and Wales to live permanently? (For legal purposes this generally means they were domiciled in England and Wales. You may wish to seek legal advice about this.)

☐ Yes

☐ No

Note 2.8 – Living permanently means they had either their permanent or principal home in England and Wales at the date of death or they intended to return to England and Wales to live permanently.

2.9 What was the marital status of the person who has died when they died?

☐ Never married

☐ Widowed, their lawful spouse or civil partner having died before them

☐ Married/in a civil partnership - give date

☐ Divorced/civil partnership is dissolved - give date

☐ Judicially separated - give date

Note 2.9 – a civil partnership is a same-sex relationship that has been registered in accordance with the Civil Partnership Act 2004. A marriage is a legal ceremony conducted in UK under the Marriage Acts 1949, 1994 and The Marriage (Same Sex Marriage) Act 2013 or under legislation in any other country by the law applicable there. Date of divorce - this date is on their Decree Absolute, Decree of Dissolution of Partnership or Decree of Judicial Separation. You can get an official copy of these documents from the court that issued them, or from The Divorce Absolute Search Section, Central Family Court, 42–49 High Holborn, London WC1V 6NP.

2.10 What is the name of the court where the Decree Absolute, Decree of Dissolution of Partnership or Decree of Judicial Separation was issued?

2.11 Did the person who has died own any foreign assets?

☐ Yes, the total value of their foreign assets (not including houses or land)

£

☐ No

12 Was there any land vested in the person who has died which was settled previously to their death and which remained settled land not withstanding their death?

☐ Yes

☐ No

Note 2.12 – It is rare for estates to be subject to the provisions of the Settled Land Act 1925 but if you know this applies or have any queries please seek legal advice.

Only answer this question if no executor to the will is applying

13 Was the person who has died or any of their relatives legally adopted in or out of the family?

☐ Yes, **see note 2.13**

☐ No, **go to question 3**

Note 2.13 – If you answered Yes to this question we may require additional information to be submitted once we have received your application.

14 Please name the legally adopted relatives and give their relationship to the person who has died. Please state whether they were adopted into the family of the person who has died, or 'adopted out' (become part of someone else's family).

Name	Relationship	Adopted in or out

3. The will and any codicils – This section is about the will. You must submit the most recent original will and codicils made since the last will, if there are any.

3.1 What is the date of the will you are submitting to the court?

[| | | | |]

3.2 Did the person who has died also leave any codicils, made since that will?

☐ Yes, **please provide the original document(s) with your application and list below the dates of the codicils you are submitting to the court.**

[| | | | |]

[| | | | |]

[| | | | |]

[| | | | |]

[| | | | |]

☐ No

3.3 Did the person who has died have any wills that were made outside of England and Wales?

☐ Yes

☐ No

3.4 Did the person who has died marry or enter into a Civil Partnership after the date of the will or any codicils?

☐ Yes, please give the date of marriage or civil partnership

[| | | | |]

☐ No

Only answer this question if no executor to the will is applying

3.5 Is there anyone under 18 years old who receives a gift in the will or a codicil?

☐ Yes, **Please note two applicants will need to apply in Section A. Contact HMCTS Probate to see who is entitled to make the application.**

☐ No

Note 3 – a will does not have to be a formal document. Please make sure you send the original will with your application. If you do not then this will delay your application.

If you have been unable to locate the original will or any codicil and only have a copy and have made all reasonable attempts to locate the original. Please visit GOV. UK (gov.uk/wills-probate-inheritance/if-the-person-left a-will) to print off the PA13 lost will questionnaire or call 0117 9302430 and quote 'Lost will' and we will supply additional information to help you proceed.

Note 3.2 – a codicil is a document that amends a will

6 Name any executors who are **not** making this application, and explain why.

Reasons for executors not applying:

A – They died before the person who has died.

B – They died after the person who has died (Please include the date they died by their name).

C – Power reserved: they have chosen not to apply, but reserve the right to do so later.

D – Renunciation: they have chosen not to apply, and give up all rights to apply. (Before you send off your application please **read NOTE REASON D**)

E – Power of attorney: they have appointed or wish to appoint another person to act as their attorney to take a Grant of Representation on their behalf (You will also need to complete Section 5 of this application). (Before you send off your application please **read NOTE REASON E**)

F – They lack capacity to act as executor.

Full name(s) of executor(s) **not** applying	A, B, C, D, E or F

Note 3.6 – Executors are the first person who can apply for a grant. We need to know why any executors aren't included in this application. This includes any executors who have pre-deceased. **If you do not provide all of the information this will delay your application.**

Reason C

If any executors are having power reserved, you **must** notify them of the application in writing. The Grant of Representation will only be issued to those people named as applicants in Section A.

Reason D

If you state that an executor has given up their right to apply. We need to send another form to you to give to the executor, or them to sign. Please visit GOV.UK (gov.uk/wills-probate-inheritance/if-youre-an-executor) to print off the PA15 renunciation form or call 0117 9302430 and quote 'Renunciation' and we will send the renunciation form.

You will need to send the renunciation form to us with this application.

Reason E

If you state that an executor wishes to appoint an attorney or they already have an attorney. We will need to send another form to you to give to the executor for them to sign, or you will need to provide one of the forms mentioned in Section 5.

Please visit GOV.UK (gov.uk/wills-probate-inheritance/if-youre-an-executor) to print off the PA11 attorney form or call 0117 9302430 and quote 'Attorney' and we will send the attorney form.

You will need to send the attorney form to us with this application. The attorney of one executor and an executor acting in their own right may not jointly apply for a Grant of Representation.

Reason F

If you state that an executor lacks capacity and are incapable of managing their property and financial affairs, when we receive this application we may send a medical certificate for the executors' doctor to sign. If you do not already have medical evidence from a qualified practitioner or are using a registered LPA a short form of medical evidence will be required.

Please visit GOV.UK (gov.uk/wills-probate-inheritance/if-youre-an-executor) to print off the PA14 medical certificate or call 0117 9302430 and quote 'Medical evidence' and we will send out the form.

You will need to send the medical certificate to us with this application.

The attorney of one executor and an executor acting in their own right may not jointly apply for a Grant of Representation.

3.7 ☐ The undersigned declare that written notice has been given to all executors who have power reserved to them and are not making this application.

If you fail to give written notice, it is likely to delay your application.

3.8 Did you separate the will for photocopying purposes?

☐ Yes - please explain the details in the box below including who separated it, when they did and why they did it.

☐ No

3.9 Can you confirm the will consisted of the pages now being submitted and no other pages or documents of a testamentary nature or other nature were attached.

☐ Yes

☐ No

Relatives of the person who has died

1 Did the person who has died leave a surviving spouse or civil partner?

☐ Yes

☐ No

Note 4.1 – 'survive' means that they were alive when the deceased person died.

2 How many of the following blood and adoptive relatives did the person who has died have?

Note 4.2 – Please state the **number** of relatives the person who has died had in the relevant sections. If none then put nil or strike through.

	Under 18 years	Over 18 years
a How many sons or daughters of the person who died survived them?		
b How many sons or daughters of the person who has died who did not survive them?		
c How many children of people at 'b' who survived them?		

3 Please state the relationship of each of the persons applying for the grant to the person who has died. (If you are applying as an attorney for someone then please state attorney)

Relationship description

First applicant

Second applicant

Third applicant

Fourth applicant

5. Applying as an attorney

5.1 Are you applying as an attorney on behalf of one or more people who are entitled to apply for a Grant of Representation?

☐ Yes, **go to question 5.2**

☐ No, **go to section 6**

5.2 Please give the full names of the person or people on whose behalf you are applying.

5.3 Please give their address

Building and street

Second line of address

Town or city

County (optional)

Postcode

5.4 Is a person on whose behalf you are applying unable to make a decision for themselves due to an impairment of or a disturbance in the functioning of their mind or brain?

☐ Yes, further confirmation of this will be requested by HMCTS Probate.

☐ No

5.5 Has anyone been appointed by the Court of Protection to act on behalf of a person on whose behalf you are applying including the right for a grant of representation?

☐ Yes, **please provide an official copy of the court order with your application**

☐ No

Note 5 – if you are applying on behalf of more than one person, please provide the information requested in this section for the other people you represent on a separate sheet of paper. We will need to send another form to you to give to the executor for them to sign, or you will need to provide one of the forms mentioned in this section.

Please visit GOV.UK (gov.uk/ wills-probate-inheritance/ if-youre-an-executor) to print off the PA11 attorney form or call 0117 9302430 and quote 'Attorney' and we will send the attorney form.

You will need to send the signed attorney form to us with this application. The attorney of one executor and an executor acting in their own right may not jointly apply for a Grant of Representation.

Where there are persons aged under 18 benefiting from the estate then two applicants (or at least two) will be needed in Section A. You may wish to contact HMCTS Probate to seek information in regard to who is eligible to apply.

Note 5.4 – this applies if they lack capacity under the Mental Capacity Act 2005 and are incapable of managing their property and financial affairs. You may wish to seek legal advice about this.

If you do not already have medical evidence from a qualified practitioner or are using a registered LPA a short form of medical evidence will be required.

Please visit GOV.UK (gov.uk/ wills-probate-inheritance/ if-youre-an-executor) to print off the PA14 medical certificateor call 0117 9302430 and quote 'medical evidence' and we will send the form.

6 Has a person on whose behalf you are applying appointed an attorney under an Enduring Power of Attorney (EPA) or a Property and Financial Affairs Lasting Power of Attorney (LPA)?

☐ Yes, **please provide the original EPA/LPA (or a solicitor's certified copy of it certified on every page.) with your application**

☐ No, **go to Section 6**

7 Has the Enduring Power of Attorney (EPA) been registered with the Office of the Public Guardian?

☐ Yes

☐ No

6. Foreign domicile

Note – if you answered Yes, to question 2.8 you don't need to complete this section – please go to Section 7.

6.1 What was the country where the person who died either lived permanently at the date of death or intended to return to live permanently?

6.2 What does the estate in England and Wales of the person has died consist of?

Assets	Values

6.3 Has an entrusting document been issued by the court where the person who has died was domiciled?

☐ Yes, **please provide the official document with your application; if it is not in English, please also provide an official translation. Go to Section 7.**

☐ No

6.4 Has a succession certificate, inheritance certificate or equivalent document been issued by a court or Notary in the country of domicile of the person who has died?

☐ Yes, **please provide the offical document with your application; if it is not in English, please also provide an official translation.**

☐ No

Note 6.3 and 6.4 – these documents may help to support your application. If you do not have any of these documents, you may wish to seek legal advice.

Inheritance tax

1 Did you complete an Inheritance Tax Estate report online?

☐ Yes, do not submit an Inheritance Tax form with this application

   Please provide the following details, **then go to Legal Statement:**

   IHT Identifier [   ]

   Gross Estate Figure £ [   ]

   Net Estate Figure £ [   ]

☐ No, **go to question 7.2**

2 Which of the following inheritance tax forms have you completed?

☐ Form **IHT205, complete 7.3 then go to Legal Statement**

☐ Form **IHT207, complete 7.4 then go to Legal Statement**

☐ Forms **IHT400** and **IHT421, complete 7.5 then go to Legal Statement**

3 Provide the following figures from form **IHT205.**

   Figure from box D £ [   ]

   Figure from box F £ [   ]
   (This figure will determine
   the probate application fee)

4 Provide the following figures from form **IHT207.**

   Figure from box A £ [   ]

   Figure from box H £ [   ]
   (This figure will determine
   the probate application fee)

5 Provide the following figures from form **IHT421.**

   Figure from box 3 £ [   ]
   (Gross value of assets)

   Figure from box 5 £ [   ]
   (Net value)

   (This figure will determine
   the probate application fee)

Note 7 – if you completed an Inheritance Tax Summary online, and fully complete question 7.1 of this form, you do not need to send an Inheritance Tax Estate report form with your application.

For guidance on probate fees please visit www. gov.uk/wills-probate-inheritance/

Note 7.2 – if you did not complete an Inheritance Tax Estate report online, you **must** complete IHT205, or IHT207, or both IHT400 and IHT421.

Note 7.3 – if the person who has died, died before 1 September 2006, it may affect which tax form you need to complete, so please ring the **Probate Helpline** on **0300 123 1072.**

Note 7.5 – do **not** send form IHT400 or form IHT421 to us. Please send them to HM Revenue and Customs, Inheritance Tax, BX9 1HT, at the same time you send PA1P and other papers to HMCTS Probate. HMRC will stamp your IHT421 and send it to HMCTS Probate.

LEGAL STATEMENT

The undersigned confirms:

- That the last will and any codicils referred to in this application is the last will and testament of the person who has died
- to collect the whole estate
- to keep full details (an inventory) of the estate
- to keep a full account of how the estate has been distributed

If HMCTS Probate (court) asks the undersigned they will:

- Provide the full details of the estate and how it has been distributed
- Return the grant of representation to the court

and understand that:

- The application will be rejected if the information is not provided (if asked)
- Criminal proceedings for fraud may be brought against the undersigned if it is found that the evidence provided is deliberately untruthful or dishonest

The undersigned confirm to administer the estate of the person who has died in accordance to law, and that the application is truthful.

ALL PERSONS APPLYING FOR THE GRANT (those listed in Section A) **MUST SIGN BELOW.**

Name of **first applicant**	Name of **second applicant**
Signature	Signature
Date signed	Date signed

Name of **third applicant**	Name of **fourth applicant**
Signature	Signature
Date signed	Date signed

Please see leaflet PA4SOT for where to make your payment and send your completed form.

Phone 0300 303 0648
Email contactprobate@justice.gov.uk

ow are the applicants entitled to apply.

In what capacity are the persons applying entitled to apply?

☐ The executor/s named in the will/codicil of the person who has died

☐ The Attorney/s acting on behalf of the executor/s named in the will/codicil of the person who has died

☐ Beneficiary/s named in the will/codicil of the person who has died

☐ The Attorney/s acting on behalf of the beneficiary/s named in the will/codicil of the person who has died

☐ Other (Please state in the box below the reason they are applying)

How to apply for probate –

A guide for people applying without a solicitor

Applying for the legal right to deal with someone's property, money and possessions (their 'estate') when they die is called 'applying for probate'.

If the person left a will, you'll get a 'grant of probate'. If the person did not leave a will, you'll get 'letters of administration'.

You may not need probate if the person who died:

- had jointly owned land, property, shares or money – they will automatically pass to the surviving owners
- only had small savings or premium bonds

Contact each asset holder (for example a bank or mortgage company) to find out if you'll need probate to get access to assets. Every organisation has its own rules.

You can order extra copies of the probate document so you can send it to different organisations at the same time.

The process is different in Scotland and Northern Ireland. Contact the inheritance tax and probate helpline for advice.

Who can apply

If the person left a will

You can apply if you're an executor – someone named in the will, or in an update to the will (a 'codicil'), as a person who can deal with the estate.

You need the will and any updates to apply. These must be original documents, not photocopies.

The person who died should have told all executors where to find the original will, for example:

- at their house
- with a solicitor
- at the London Probate Department – you'll need the death certificate and to prove you're the executor to be sent the will

If the person did not leave a will

You can apply for letters of administration if you're the person's next of kin, in the following order of priority:

1. the married partner or civil partner
2. their child (including adopted children, but not step-children)
3. their parent
4. their brother or sister
5. their grandparent
6. their uncle or aunt

You can apply if you were still married or in a civil partnership with the person when they died, even if you were separated from them.

You cannot apply if you're the partner of the person but were not their spouse or civil partner when they died.

Joint applications

Usually only one person needs to apply for probate.

If more than one person is named as an executor, you must all agree who makes the application for probate. Up to 4 people can apply. If only one executor applies they'll need to prove they tried to contact all executors.

If the person entitled to the estate is under 18 two people are legally required to apply.

Only the executors who make the application will be named on the grant and their signatures will be needed to release the assets of the person who died.

If you do not want to or cannot be an executor

The will may name a replacement executor for someone who becomes 'unwilling or unable' to deal with the estate. Contact your local probate registry if no executors are willing or able to apply for probate.

You do not want to be an executor

You can do one of the following:

- give up your right to apply for probate (known as 'renunciation') – fill in a renunciation form (PA15) and send it with your probate application (PA1P)
- reserve your right to apply for probate later if another executor cannot deal with the estate (holding 'power reserved')
- appoint an attorney to act on your behalf – fill in an attorney form (PA11) and send it with your probate application, or send a signed Enduring Power of Attorney (EPA) or Lasting Power of Attorney (LPA)

A Lasting Power of Attorney must be registered with the Office of the Public Guardian.

When an executor is unable to apply for probate

A replacement executor should apply for probate if the executor is unable to, for example because:

- they've died
- they do not have 'mental capacity' – get a doctor to fill in a medical certificate form (PA14) and send it with the probate application

How to apply for probate

Report the estate's value and pay any inheritance tax you owe

You must estimate and report the estate's value to HM Revenue & Customs (HMRC) before you apply for probate.

How to do this:

- online – complete an Inheritance Tax Estate Report at www.tax.service.gov.uk/inheritance-tax
- by post if there is Inheritance Tax to pay – complete the inheritance tax account form (IHT400)
- by post if there is no Inheritance Tax to pay – complete the return of estate information form (IHT205)

Depending on estate's value, you may have to pay Inheritance Tax. You normally have to pay at least some of it before you're given probate. You can claim the tax back from the estate or beneficiaries if you pay it out of your own bank account.

Apply for probate online

Go to www.apply-for-probate.service.gov.uk to apply online. You can use this service if you're the executor and you:

- have the original will (if the person who died left a will)
- have the Official death certificate (or an interim certificate) from the coroner

Apply for probate by post

If the person who died left a will, fill in the probate application form PA1P. If they did not leave a will, fill in form PA1A.

Send it to your local probate registry along with your documents. See the directory of probate registries (leaflet PA4) for the postal address.

Sending documents

If you apply online you'll be told which documents to send and where to send them.

If you apply by post you'll need to send these documents to your local probate registry along with your application form:

- the original will and any updates
- the official death certificate or an interim death certificate from the coroner

The registry will not return the original will as it becomes part of public record.

You may want to make copies for your own records. Do not remove any staples or bindings to make copies.

Payment

See the probate fees list (PA3) for application costs.

If you apply online you'll pay by debit or credit card.

If you apply by post you can:

- send a cheque payable to HM Courts & Tribunals Service with your documents
- call the probate registry and pay by debit or credit card – you'll be given a reference number to send with your documents.

After you've applied

You'll receive the grant of probate and any copies you've ordered within 20 working days of your documents being received.

The Probate Registry will send you a letter or email you if they need any more information.

Get help

Probate helpline

0300 303 0648

Welsh language helpline

0845 302 1489

Opening hours

Monday to Friday, 9am to 5pm

Useful links:

- Information on applying for probate www.gov.uk/wills-probate-inheritance
- Probate forms and leaflets www.hmctsformfinder.justice.gov.uk
- Addresses of regional probate registries courttribunalfinder.service.gov.uk
- Information on inheritance tax www.hmrc.gov.uk/inheritancetax

Probate forms and leaflets

PA1P	Apply for probate (deceased left a will) (form)
PA1A	Apply for probate (deceased did not leave a will) (form)
PA2	How to apply for probate (leaflet)
PA3	Probate fees list (leaflet)
PA4	Directory of probate registries and interview venues (leaflet)
PA7	How to deposit a will with the probate service (leaflet)
PA7A	Withdrawing your will from the principal Probate Registry (form)
PA8	How to enter a caveat (leaflet)
PA8A	Apply to enter a caveat (form)
PA11	Apply for power of attorney (form)
PA1S	Apply for a probate search or standing search (form)
PA14	Medical certificate (form)
PA15	Apply for renunciation (form)
PA97	Notice to personal applicant

HMRC Inheritance Tax forms

IHT205	Return of estate information
IHT206	Return of estate information (guidance notes)
IHT400	Inheritance Tax Account
IHT400	Guidance notes

Probate Fees from July 2019

	Fee
Application In all cases where the net estate (ie the amount remaining in the deceased's sole name after funeral expenses and debts owing have been deducted) is **over £5,000** (see example 1 below). **Note: Joint assets passing automatically to the surviving joint owner should not be included when calculating the fee.**	£215
If the net estate as above is **under £5,000** (see example 2 below).	No fee
Application for a second grant in an estate where a previous grant has been issued.	£20
Additional Copies Official (sealed) copies of the Grant of Representation **if** ordered when you lodge your application for a Grant of Representation. **Note: You should decide how many copies you will need and add the cost to your application fee – this will give you the total amount payable. See examples below. It can save you a lot of time when collecting in the deceased's assets if you have a few extra copies of the grant to produce to the organisations holding the assets.**	£1.50 per copy
'Sealed and certified copy' – if assets are held abroad you may need one of these. Please check with the appropriate organisations before ordering.	£1.50 per copy (including Will and Grant)
Additional copies (consisting of grant including a copy of the Will, if applicable) ordered after the Grant of Representation has been issued.	£1.50 per copy

Example 1				**Example 2**			
Net estate of £75,000	=	Fee	£215	Net estate of £2,000	=	Fee	Nil
4 copies of grant at	=	Fee	£ 6	1 copy of grant at	=	Fee	£1.50
£1.50 each		Total Fee	£221	£1.50 each		Total Fee	£1.50

Please send a cheque or postal order (no cash) made payable to '**HM Courts & Tribunals Service**', together with your application forms, to the Probate Registry to which you are applying. You should state the number and type of copies you need on the checklist on page 1 of the probate application form (PA1A/PA1P). Please print the name of the **deceased person** on the back of the cheque.

Please ensure you order sufficient copies for your needs, when you send in your application.

Please note: Appropriate post must be paid. (Standard rate postage may not be sufficient. If your forms weigh over 60g they may need to be weighed at your local Post Office.)

What if I cannot afford to pay a fee?

If you cannot afford the fee, you may be eligible for a fee remission in full or part. The combined booklet and application form EX160A - Court fees - do I have to pay them? gives all the information you need. You can get a copy from any Probate Registry or from our website www.hmcourts-service.gov.uk.

Your application will not be processed until the fee is paid (or an application for refund/remission has been successful).

Index

**